NATURAL GAS REGULATION

THE AEI
NATIONAL ENERGY PROJECT

The American Enterprise Institute's
National Energy Project was established in early 1974
to examine the broad array of issues
affecting U.S. energy demands and supplies.
The project will commission research into all important
ramifications of the energy problem—economic
and political, domestic and international, private
and public—and will present the results
in studies such as this one.
In addition it will sponsor symposia, debates, conferences,
and workshops, some of which will be televised.

The project is chaired by Melvin R. Laird,
former congressman, secretary of defense,
and domestic counsellor to the President,
and now senior counsellor of *Reader's Digest.*
An advisory council, representing a wide range of
energy-related viewpoints, has been appointed.
The project director is Edward J. Mitchell,
professor of business economics at
the University of Michigan.

Views expressed are those of the authors
and do not necessarily reflect the views of
either the advisory council and others associated with
the project or of the advisory panels,
staff, officers, and trustees of AEI.

NATURAL GAS REGULATION
An evaluation of FPC price controls
Robert B. Helms

American Enterprise Institute for Public Policy Research
Washington, D. C.

Robert B. Helms, formerly assistant professor of economics at
Loyola College, Baltimore, is a senior staff member of the
American Enterprise Institute.

ISBN 0-8447-3136-6

National Energy Study 2, July 1974

Library of Congress Catalog Card No. 74-84019

Printed in the United States of America

CONTENTS

FIGURES

FOREWORD

This volume is the second in a series of monographs on U.S. energy policy sponsored by the AEI National Energy Project. While the project has been in existence only a few months, it is expected there will now be a continuous flow of new studies released to the public just as quickly as the review and publication process permits. Energy policy is being made every day. Only by providing information to the public and to government on a current basis can policy making be assisted and improved.

This monograph on natural gas price regulation is especially timely. The nation is in the throes of debate on the role of federal price controls on fuels. On the one hand, some argue that, in view of sharply escalating prices in the past year, a more comprehensive system of strict price controls is needed. On the other hand, it is argued that price controls are in large part responsible for shortages of domestic fuel and our heavy reliance on expensive oil imports. We now have a fourteen-year historical experience with federal price controls on what is currently our largest domestic source of energy—natural gas. To ignore that history and its lessons would be folly.

I am sure the reader will find Dr. Helms's study a valuable contribution to the discussion.

Edward J. Mitchell
Project Director

INTRODUCTION:
THE EXAMPLE OF
NATURAL GAS REGULATION

The natural gas producer market, which supplies gas to interstate pipelines in the field (at the wellhead), has been under price controls for approximately thirteen years. Field price regulation was set up to protect consumers from higher prices.[1] This it apparently has done at least for some consumers for part of the period since 1960.

But these savings for a subset of consumers have had their costs. There now is a shortage of natural gas. The Federal Power Commission (FPC) has been forced to establish a rationing system to allocate existing supplies of gas. Some consumers unable to obtain gas are paying higher prices for substitute fuels—but in the absence of regulation they could have had gas at prices lower than those paid for the substitute fuels. Even those now obtaining gas from distributors are finding their costs rising more rapidly than would have been the case in an unregulated market. An increasing portion of the Boston supply, for example, consists of liquefied natural gas (LNG) selling at $1.58/Mcf because not enough domestic natural gas can be obtained at the 67¢/Mcf "city gate" (retail) price.[2] An 80¢/Mcf city gate price would have increased domestic supplies

This study is based on the model and results from my dissertation (UCLA, 1973). I am deeply grateful to my dissertation committee chairman, Professor Sam Peltzman, for his guidance and help. I would also like to thank Professor Yale Brozen for his invaluable assistance in the preparation of this study, as well as Professor Edward J. Mitchell and Dr. J. Rhodes Foster for their helpful comments and suggestions. Sole responsibility for the contents or any remaining mistakes in the study is, of course, mine.

[1] § 4, 15 U.S.C. § 717 (c); Atlantic Refining Co. v. Public Service Commission of New York (CATCO), 360 U.S. 378, 388 (1959).

[2] *Natural Gas Policy Issues and Options,* Senate Committee on Interior and Insular Affairs, Serial No. 93-20 (Washington, D.C.: Government Printing Office, 1973), p. 3.

sufficiently to have made the importation of $1.58/Mcf LNG unnecessary and would have resulted in a lower Boston price in the long run.

To many people, the natural gas shortage is just another aspect of the "energy crisis." In one sense, they are correct. New consumers cannot obtain gas and some old consumers have been "curtailed," and both have turned to the use of oil. Because of the resulting increased demand for heating oil, gasoline production has been curtailed. Under price control, shortages of gasoline and heating oil appeared even before the Middle East war of October 1973 and the Arab boycott. But shortages of natural gas and "curtailments" began at least two years before the heating oil difficulties of the winter of 1971-72. The roots of the shortage of natural gas reach back a long way.

This situation is now the subject of extended congressional hearings to determine if a shortage really exists and, if it does, what caused it. President Nixon has responded to popular concern by introducing a packet of bills proposing, among other things, excess profit taxes and increased reporting requirements for energy producing companies.[3] Among some congressmen there is now talk that protection of consumers requires public utility regulation for the oil industry.[4]

To the student of natural gas regulation, this has a familiar ring. In a 1968 article, Edmund W. Kitch discussed the response to the shortage of natural gas and the resulting increase in prices which occurred in the Appalachian producing area during the early 1920s.[5] The Appalachian market was under state public utility regulation which controlled intrastate prices in the face of growing demand and limited production capacity. Shortages occurred in the Appalachian area at the same time that large discoveries were made in Kansas and the Texas Panhandle, but this was before the development of long-distance pipelines which could bring gas to the areas where there were shortages. The conditions in these two areas were discussed in a Federal Trade Commission report which became the basis for the Natural Gas Act of 1938.[6] However, as Kitch pointed out:

---

[3] Radio Energy Message to the Nation, January 19, 1974.

[4] Nationalization of the oil industry has also been mentioned.

[5] Edmund W. Kitch, "Regulation of the Field Market for Natural Gas," Journal of Law and Economics, vol. 11 (October 1968), pp. 248-254.

[6] Final Report of the FTC on Utility Corporations, S. Doc. 92, 70th Congress, 1st session (1936).

2

. . . the Natural Gas Act responded only to the problems of the Appalachian fields; . . . The FTC Report found the cause of the problem in the Appalachian fields to be not a declining supply, about which nothing could be done, but the "monopolies" of the interstate pipeline holding companies who were free to raise their prices without regard to the consumer interest. The response was a traditional utility rate base regulatory scheme applicable to interstate pipeline operations.[7]

The extension of regulatory authority to the field market (discussed in Chapter 2) was essentially a congressional response to rising prices in the 1950s. These rising prices were essentially the result of (1) a large increase in demand for field gas as gas markets were extended over most of the United States and (2) declining monopsony (buyer control of price) and increased competition among pipelines for field purchases.

The two major extensions of regulatory authority in the natural gas market have been made in periods of rising gas prices despite the fact that it was buyers who bid up the price of gas in order to obtain a fuel that (even with the price bid up) was cheaper and more convenient than alternative fuels. In effect, producers of alternative fuels were protected against the increased availability of natural gas which would have been the natural result of higher prices. In the short run, it may have appeared to many of these producers that they were being hurt by the ceilings on natural gas prices in the field; but in the long run, those ceilings protected them.

We have now experienced an increase in the price of crude petroleum. To the extent that FPC policy permits it, an increase in the price of natural gas is also occurring. Public and congressional clamor to "do something" in both industries is considerable. Additional controls and public utility-type regulation are being proposed for major oil companies. Also, there are proposals to extend natural gas regulation to the now unregulated intrastate natural gas market. It is claimed this would be the way to force natural gas producers to sell more of their gas to the interstate market (and less to the intrastate market).

With these proposals being discussed, it is imperative that a careful study of the effects of previous regulation be made. Because crude oil and natural gas are produced jointly in many regions of the United States and because there are many similarities in the exploration, development, and production of the two products, the lessons

[7] Kitch, "Regulation of Field Market," p. 254.

to be learned from our thirteen-year experience with natural gas regulation can reasonably be transferred to the crude oil producing industry.

A study of the controls of field market prices established by the FPC in the 1960s also permits us to assess the longer-term effects of price controls on producers' expectations, the supply of natural gas, and the administrative burden on the regulatory agency. Price controls on nonpublic-utility industries are a relatively new form of peace-time economic regulation for this country. While traditional public utility regulation has been subject to detailed study and analysis, the U.S. experiment with natural gas field market regulation gives us a chance to analyze the effects of regulation on an industry of a more competitive structure.

The study is organized in the following way. Chapters 1 and 2 provide background information on the structure, organization, and history of the industry and its regulation. Chapter 3 outlines a model used to predict the way producers could have been expected to behave in the absence of FPC regulation. The model's projections of several supply variables are presented and discussed. In the light of these projections, Chapter 4 evaluates several aspects of FPC policy designed to protect consumers and to stimulate exploration and development of new supplies. Chapter 5 provides recommendations for future public policy toward the field market for natural gas.

The main conclusion of the study is that thirteen years of experience with field market regulation in the United States provides an example of an unsuccessful attempt to improve social welfare through price controls. Shortages of natural gas are a direct consequence of these price controls. Deregulation of the field market would reduce this country's future energy costs.

1

ORGANIZATION AND HISTORY OF THE NATURAL GAS INDUSTRY

Natural gas is a simple hydrocarbon of the paraffin series which is gaseous when brought to the surface. It can take any of the following three forms: (1) dry gas, consisting of methane or ethane, (2) LP-gas, consisting of propane or butane, and (3) natural gasoline, consisting of pentane, hexane, heptane, and octane.[1] Methane is the most common form of natural gas and ethane the next most common. Almost all commercially used gas is dry gas yielding about 1,000 BTU per cubic foot. On a BTU basis, natural gas now supplies approximately one-third of U.S. energy.

The common unit for natural gas is the Mcf—1,000 cubic feet. Larger quantities are expressed as:

Bcf—"billion cubic feet," equal to 1,000,000 Mcf, or

Tcf—"trillion cubic feet," equal to 1,000,000,000 Mcf.

The natural gas industry in the United States may be divided into three broad categories: the field market, the pipelines, and the distribution markets. The field market is the market for gas at the wellhead. Producers of natural gas search out and develop natural gas reserves and then contract with a pipeline company to deliver gas to the company over some time period. Generally, the pipeline companies, which link the field and distribution markets, do not usually act as common carriers. Rather, they purchase gas in the field, transport it to market and sell it, either to distribution companies for resale or directly to industrial customers. Distribution companies are usually local public utilities that sell gas to residential, commercial, and industrial customers.

---

[1] John R. Stockton, Richard C. Henshaw, Jr., and Richard W. Graves, *Economics of Natural Gas in Texas* (Austin: University of Texas, 1952).

The Field Market for Natural Gas

This study is primarily concerned with the regulation of the field market for natural gas. To understand the behavior of those participating in this market, it will be helpful to consider how and where natural gas is found.

As gas is formed from the decomposition of organic materials, it seeps through small openings or pores until it encounters a layer of nonporous rock. There it accumulates in "traps." A "field" consists of a group of such traps, occurring near each other or in layers above and below each other.

When gas is found in the same trap with oil, it is called either "dissolved gas," meaning it is in solution with oil, or "associated gas," meaning the gas occurs in a layer above a layer of oil. Gas found alone is called "nonassociated" gas. In the past decade, approximately 70 percent of proven reserves of natural gas have been nonassociated gas.[2]

Although terminology differs, the production of natural gas will be used here to mean the entire process of locating and extracting natural gas from the geological traps which contain it. Production is traditionally divided into three activities: exploration, development, and extraction. Exploration and development refer to the process of producing (finding and delineating) reserves of natural gas. Extraction refers to the process of depleting reserves and delivering the product into a pipeline or processing plant.

Exploration is essentially a process of gathering information about the location of reserves and involves geological and geophysical surveys, aerial surveys, and the drilling of exploratory wells. Only about 15 to 20 percent of all exploratory wells are successful,[3] but even "dry holes" produce information about the probable location of gas reserves. This has resulted in the gas-field institution of "dry-hole money," an arrangement whereby producers agree to share the drilling expenses in the event a well is unsuccessful in exchange for information. As Professor Adelman points out, there is no time period for exploration that can logically be called the long run because there is no way of predicting when the information produced by a dry well will become useful.[4] Geological informa-

---

[2] FPC, *A Staff Report on National Gas Supply and Demand* (Washington, D. C.: Bureau of Natural Gas, 1969), Table 6.

[3] FPC, *National Gas Supply and Demand, 1971-1990* (Washington, D. C.: Bureau of Natural Gas, February 1972), Table 18. The percentage of successful wells declined from 19.8 percent in 1959 to 16.5 percent by 1970.

[4] M. A. Adelman, *The Supply and Price of Natural Gas* (Oxford: Basil Blackwell, 1962).

6

tion may be obtained from core samples from a dry well, and this information may become valuable when combined with additional information produced years later. This makes it difficult to associate any one year's expenditure on exploration with an "output" of reserves.

Some of the exploratory activity for gas is conducted jointly with the search for crude oil. This leads to joint cost problems in defining and measuring the cost of exploration for gas. Considerable testimony given in the Permian Basin area rate hearings centered on the effect of price regulation on the search for gas. The dispute revolved around the "directionality" of gas search.

Before the development of the pipeline system connecting natural gas-producing areas with extensive markets, gas had a low market value and was commonly "vented" or "flared" at the well. Gas was found almost exclusively as a result of the search for oil. If this were still the case, it could be argued that the regulation of the price of natural gas would have little effect on the discovery of gas reserves. However, if "directionality" exists in the search for gas, then regulation should influence future gas supplies. Given that the probabilities of finding gas or oil differ by location and geological formation, and that approximately 70 percent of all gas is nonassociated, there seems to be both logical and empirical support for directionality in the search for gas. Even for associated gas, a higher price encourages the search for oil and associated gas and leads to the greater production of gas reserves.

One successful exploratory well usually does not provide sufficient information for the completion of a sales contract with a pipeline company. The pipeline company requires delivery of a specified volume at a uniform annual rate for a relatively long period (usually fifteen to twenty years). If the producer believes the new discovery to be commercial, he will begin to drill "step-out" wells over the expected reservoir in order to define its limits and reach a better estimate of "reserves in place" and the cost of extraction. "Step-out" drilling begins the development phase—defined roughly as that phase which delineates the potential of a discovery already made. Usually 20 to 40 percent of the wells drilled in a producing field are drilled during this "step-out" phase. These wells provide sufficient information to negotiate a contract with a buyer.

The third production activity is extraction, the process of moving gas from the reservoir into a pipeline or processing plant. Given sufficient pressure differential between underground gas and the pipeline, gas flows into the pipeline without the use of pumping equipment. Professor MacAvoy suggests that about 50 percent of reserves are recovered through this pressure differential.[5] Professor Hawkins divides extraction costs into three subcategories: (1) pumping and other lifting costs, (2) field maintenance and upkeep items, and (3) continuing expenditures on land-use agreements.[6]

Extraction, according to Adelman, is like other economic activity in that current inputs are closely related to current output, and unit costs can be computed.[7] This is not the case with exploration and development, he argues, though a more precise approximation of costs can be derived for development than for exploration. But even given the more accurate unit costs obtainable for extraction, extraction is relatively uninteresting. It is unresponsive to economic changes because there is little managerial discretion involved. Due to constantly falling pressure, output from existing wells is always declining and extraction costs are increasing. A well is "shut-in" when the market price falls below (and is expected to stay below) current extraction costs.

Because of the uncertainty involved in exploration, the random nature of exploratory "output," and the fixed nature of extraction cost, Adelman argues that the development stage is most amenable to the study of price-cost-output behavior, even though it may not ultimately be the most important stage. Cost estimates for gas and oil indicate that development expenditures account for a little more than one-third of total production expenditures, with exploration and extraction each accounting for slightly less than one-third.[8]

Until recent years, the discovery of natural gas reserves was closely related to the development of the oil industry. Before 1890, the use of natural gas was restricted to the Appalachian area from Kentucky to western New York. Use expanded into the "gas belt" of Ohio and Indiana when gas was discovered there. As the search for oil grew in the Southwest, gas was discovered with the oil, but it was considered a nuisance and was often "flared" or "vented."

Major discoveries greatly increasing the supply of reserves in the Southwest were the Monroe Field in Louisiana (1916), the Panhandle Field in Texas (1918), the Hugoton Field extending from northern Texas to southwest Kansas (1922), and the Carthage Field in Texas (1936). Many smaller discoveries were also made in

---

[5] Paul W. MacAvoy, *Price Formation in Natural Gas Fields* (New Haven: Yale University Press, 1962), p. 12.

[6] Clark A. Hawkins, *The Field Price Regulation of Natural Gas* (Tallahassee: The Florida State University Press, 1970), p. 87.

[7] Adelman, *Supply and Price of Natural Gas*, p. 3.

[8] Hawkins, *Field Price Regulation*, p. 87.

eastern Texas and the Gulf Coast areas.[9] But it was not until the construction of long-distance pipelines in the 1920s that a substantial market began to develop. As the consumption of gas became more dispersed, Texas, Louisiana, Oklahoma, Kansas, and New Mexico became more important in the production of gas. By 1960, these states accounted for 89.3 percent of reserves and 87.2 percent of marketed production.[10]

The extent to which the field market for natural gas is competitive has been the source of considerable debate, testimony, and study,[11] and it is a very live issue in the current discussions.[12] The FPC has estimated that 5,600 producers sold gas in interstate commerce in 1960 and 3,745 in 1971.[13] Hawkins has found that the largest twenty-two sellers of interstate gas sold 55.4 percent of interstate gas in 1961 and 65.5 percent in 1968,[14] a lower level of concentration than in the average manufacturing industry. The FPC reported that the comparable figure for 1971 interstate sales was 71 percent.[15] Sales by the single largest interstate producer have never exceeded the 9.2 percent of total interstate sales obtained by Humble Oil in 1971.[16] Hawkins concludes:

> The economic studies conducted in the late 1950's led to the conclusion that monopoly did not exist in field markets. The structure of the industry does not seem to have changed substantially since then, with the exception that the intrastate market may now be more important.[17]

Given many careful economic studies concluding that the field market is "workably competitive" and only vague assertions and

---

[9] Paul J. Garfield and Wallace F. Lovejoy, *Public Utility Economics* (Englewood Cliffs, N. J.: Prentice-Hall, 1964), p. 297.

[10] Ibid., p. 296.

[11] See Clark A. Hawkins, "Structure of the Natural Gas Producing Industry," in *Regulation of the Natural Gas Producing Industry,* ed. Keith C. Brown (Baltimore: Johns Hopkins University Press, 1972), Chapter 9, for a recent comprehensive study of structure and a summary of past studies by MacAvoy, Neuner, and Cookenboo.

[12] For example, see "Is the Natural Gas Industry Competitive? Congress Questions Contention That It Is," *New York Times,* July 1, 1973; and *Natural Gas Policy Issues and Options,* pp. 65-74.

[13] FPC, *Sales by Producers of Natural Gas to Interstate Pipeline Companies, 1971* (Washington, D. C.: Government Printing Office, 1972), p. vi.

[14] Hawkins, "Natural Gas Producing Industry," Tables 6-2 and 6-9.

[15] FPC, *Sales by Producers of Natural Gas,* p. vi.

[16] Ibid., and Hawkins, "Natural Gas Producing Industry," Tables 6-2 through 6-9.

[17] Hawkins, "Natural Gas Producing Industry," p. 160.

"beliefs" to the contrary, it seems reasonable to assume there is no significant monopoly power among producers. As discussions of cartel theory have pointed out, it is extremely difficult in the absence of legal sanctions to organize and perpetuate a successful collusive (cartel) arrangement to raise price and limit entry.[18] There is no evidence of the existence in the field market of the enforcement mechanism that would be necessary to bring about monopoly power. Indeed, as this study will show, the only group that has systematically obtained a change in price in its favor is the regulated pipeline companies. By preventing competition among regulated pipeline companies, the FPC has achieved a lower field price and thereby reduced the cost of the pipelines' interstate gas purchases.

Pipeline and Distribution Companies

In 1971 there were 103 interstate natural gas pipeline companies in operation, and these handled approximately 70 percent of all natural gas produced and marketed in the United States.[19] Of these, the seventy-seven class A and B pipelines handled all but a very small part of interstate gas shipments.[20]

Interstate pipeline companies are regulated by the FPC on a rate base/rate-of-return basis. Under this system, a schedule of rates is devised to cover yearly operating costs plus a specified rate of return on the rate base. The rate base is an accounting estimate of the depreciated value of investment in plant and equipment. The cost of gas purchased from the field market is the major item of expense used in the rate-making process. Over the last decade, this expense has been approximately 80 percent of operation and maintenance expenses and has consumed 56 percent of operating revenues for the major class A and B pipelines.[21] A change in field market prices could reasonably be expected to have a strong influence on pipeline company expenses. A 10 percent increase in field price would raise city gate prices 5.6 percent.

---

18 Armen A. Alchian and William A. Allen, *University Economics*, 3d ed. (Belmont, Calif.: Wadsworth Publishing Company, 1972), pp. 354-356.

19 FPC, *Sales by Producers of Natural Gas*, p. v.

20 FPC, *Statistics of Interstate Natural Gas Pipeline Companies, 1971* (Washington, D. C.: Government Printing Office, 1972), p. iii.

21 Ibid., Tables 12 and 13. Major class A and B pipelines are defined as those pipelines "whose combined sales for resale and gas transported (interstate) or stored for a fee exceeded 50 billion cubic feet during the preceding calendar year." This definition eliminates those A and B pipelines not primarily engaged in interstate transmission. There were thirty-one such companies in 1971. Ibid., p. vii.

The distribution of natural gas to the final consumer is carried out primarily by local distributors who buy gas from pipeline companies at city gate prices. Most distributors are classified as public utilities. They are generally regulated by state agencies using some form of rate-base regulation. The purchase of gas from the interstate pipeline at the city gate is the principal item of expense. In 1966-70 the average wellhead price of gas amounted to 15.6 percent of the average price charged for residential consumers and 51 percent of the lower average price charged for industrial consumers. It appears that any increase in field price would have a slight effect on residential consumers but a strong effect on industrial consumers.

An indication of the postwar growth of the retail markets served by pipeline and distributor companies appears in the growth of residential and commercial use. As Table 1 suggests, the rate of growth of the pipeline and distribution system was greatest during the decade after 1945. Growth started to decline in the late 1950s as retail markets started to fill up. This change in the rate of growth of retail markets had important effects on the field market. The decline in the rate of expansion of retail markets led to a decline in the demand for new gas in the field. This may be one reason contract prices for new gas in the field market started to decline about 1958, two years before FPC price ceilings were imposed.

The geographical organization of the natural gas industry is also significant. By computing the net flow of gas by state, Schanz

Table 1

CUSTOMERS SERVED BY NATURAL GAS COMPANIES, 1945-70

Year	Number of Customers (millions)	Percentage Growth
1945	11.8	—
1950	18.3	55%
1955	28.2	54
1960	33.7	20
1965	38.3	14
1970	41.9	9

Source: Bureau of Mines, *Minerals Yearbook,* various years.

11

and Frank have identified "five main pathways" connecting the major producing areas with retail markets.[22] These are

(1) from the Gulf Coast fields (Louisiana and the Texas Gulf) northeastward along the western flank of the Appalachian Mountains to the Midwest and northeastern seaboard;

(2) from the Gulf Coast fields eastward to the South and Southeast;

(3) from the inland producing areas (northern Texas, Oklahoma, Kansas) northward to the Midwest;

(4) from New Mexico and west Texas west to California; and

(5) from Oklahoma-Kansas areas into the Rocky Mountain area.

By volume the first three "pathways," which carry approximately 65 percent of marketed production to the major residential and industrial markets in the Midwest and on the eastern seaboard, are the most important. The geographical separation of major producing and consuming areas helps explain some of the political battle in Congress.[23]

Producer-Pipeline Contracts

The contract negotiated between the producer of natural gas and the pipeline company that purchases the gas for interstate shipment is of particular interest because it is the terms of this contract that the FPC attempts to control by regulation. In order to study the impact of regulation, it will be helpful to understand some of the terms of these contracts.

The FPC controls field prices of gas sold into interstate commerce under authority granted in the Natural Gas Act of 1938 as interpreted by the 1954 *Phillips* decision.[24] Under the act independent natural gas producers are considered to be natural gas companies: they are therefore required to apply for certificates of public convenience and necessity and to file rate schedules. Since the producer-pipeline contract is considered to be the producer's rate

---

[22] John J. Schanz, Jr., and Helmut J. Frank, "Natural Gas in the Future National Energy Pattern," in Brown, *Regulation of Natural Gas Producing Industry*, Chapter 1, p. 20 and Figure 1-1.

[23] For an interesting account of the political activities of the gas industry and consuming states in the 1950s, see Edith T. Carter, *Lobbying and the Natural Gas Bill* (University, Alabama: University of Alabama Press, 1962).

[24] This, and other cases, will be discussed in more detail in Chapter 2.

schedule, the FPC has the power to approve or reject a proposed price according to whether it thinks the price is "in the public interest." [25]

Producer-pipeline contracts are generally long-term contracts, covering the production of gas from the producers' land for twenty years or more. Two reasons are usually given for the existence of contracts covering such a long period: (1) the fact that pipeline construction is financed through the sale of long-term bonds, and (2) the regulatory requirements imposed on pipelines by the FPC. One of the requirements the FPC imposes for certification of new or expanded pipeline systems is that the systems show evidence of adequate reserves to supply the proposed system for a period of approximately twelve years.[26] Pipeline companies meet this requirement by showing ownership of reserves or contracts with producers sufficient to guarantee service.

It is often argued that even in the absence of commission certification requirements, producer-pipeline contracts would still be long-term contracts because of the use of bond financing for pipeline systems. The contention is that purchasers of pipeline bonds require the existence of a long-term supply of reserves as insurance that future revenues will be adequate to repay the bonds. Bonds have usually been issued with the agreement that payments from depreciation will be made into a sinking fund. If reserves are depleted faster than expected, depreciation funds may not be sufficient

---

[25] Garfield and Lovejoy, *Public Utility Economics*, pp. 329-330.

[26] The requirement is in terms of "deliverability," which is defined by the FPC as "the number of future years during which a pipeline company can meet its annual requirements for its presently certificated delivery capacity from presently committed sources of supply. . . ." FPC, *The Gas Supplies of Interstate Natural Gas Pipeline Companies, 1971* (Washington, D. C.: Government Printing Office, 1972), p. 102. The commission's deliverability requirement is twelve years for new or expanded markets but may be flexible when a pipeline can show that it has an active procurement organization and its pipelines extend into production areas in which exploration is continuing. FPC Order No. 279 (CFR 2.61 a, c).

Deliverability, as defined by the FPC, is affected by three factors: (1) the physical capabilities of the sources of gas, (2) the terms of existing gas-purchase contracts, and (3) the limitations imposed by state or federal regulatory agencies (FPC, *Gas Supplies of Pipeline Companies, 1971*, p. 102). Deliverability can be less than the commission's requirements for individual contracts because of increased production from old contracts to meet growing demands. Pipeline company estimates of deliverability—the number of years the company can meet present annual requirements from presently committed reserves—have declined steadily over the last few years as additions to pipeline reserves have declined and as pipelines have extracted larger annual volumes from existing supplies to meet growing demand (ibid., pp. 102-117).

to provide an adequate sinking fund. In such a case, funds which could be used for other purposes would have to be added to the sinking fund.[27] Given the difficulty of predicting the amount of production which may eventually be obtained from a gas reservoir and given the relatively large capital requirements for pipeline construction, it is logical to expect that producer-pipeline contracts would be for the relatively long term, although it is doubtful that they would extend as long as the fifteen to twenty years required to meet FPC certification standards.

The major points covered in contracts are "the amounts, price, and quantity of gas to be taken; the delivery, gathering, processing, and metering conditions; and the method and timing of payments." [28] An initial contract rate is specified. (This is usually taken as the best indication of "the price" of gas for analytical purposes.) The initial rate may not continue for the life of the contract if the contract includes an "escalation" clause.

Escalation clauses may be fixed or indefinite. Fixed escalation provides for automatic increases in the price for delivered gas, the most common fixed escalation clause providing for a one-cent increase every four years.[29] Fixed escalations in price may be advantageous to both buyer and seller. When production is first begun from a gas field, pressure is high and production costs are relatively low. The seller's production costs tend to increase over the life of the reservoir as pressurizing equipment is added and as wells require reworking and cleaning. The buyer (that is, the pipeline), on the other hand, faces high investment and market development costs in the early years. These tend to decline over time as markets are developed and as the pipeline is depreciated and capital invested in the pipeline is recovered.[30]

Indefinite escalation clauses are the natural result of the inability of producers to predict future events. They began to appear in contracts negotiated in the latter 1940s and became quite common in the 1950s.[31] Probably they resulted from three factors: (1) inflation during and after World War II, (2) increased state taxation of natural gas production, and (3) an improvement in the bargaining strength of the producers relative to the pipelines as the growth

[27] MacAvoy, *Price Formation*, pp. 29-30.

[28] Garfield and Lovejoy, *Public Utility Economics*, pp. 330-331.

[29] Hawkins, "Natural Gas Producing Industry," p. 160.

[30] Garfield and Lovejoy, *Public Utility Economics*, p. 331.

[31] E. J. Neuner, *The Natural Gas Industry* (Norman: University of Oklahoma Press, 1960), pp. 80-111.

in the number of pipeline companies made the field market for gas more competitive.

Because of the depression and the large quantities of new gas reserves discovered in the 1930s, most contracts before World War II were negotiated at very low fixed rates with no provision for future price increases.[32] Learning from the experiences of World War II and its aftermath, and faced with larger numbers of pipelines to bargain with, producers began to demand and receive insurance against inflation.

The most commonly used of these price escalation clauses have been the "most-favored-nation clause" (named after the tariff agreement provision) and the "redetermination clause." The favored-nation clause requires the buyer to pay the producer a price equal to the highest price paid to any other producer within a specified area either by the pipeline itself (two-party favored-nation clause) or by any buyer (third-party favored-nation clause). In addition to providing protection against inflation, this clause permits the producer to take advantage of favorable shifts in demand or supply conditions. If demand for the producer's fixed supply of gas increases, he is allowed to capture the economic rent which accrues from the increase.

The "redetermination clause" provides similar protection against unforeseen changes in market conditions or inflation. This clause spells out the conditions under which either party may reopen negotiations regarding the price to be paid for the gas, generally specifying the timing of redetermination and methods for arbitration.

The less used "price index" and "spiral escalation" clauses refer respectively to proportional adjustment of the field price to increases in a price index (usually the BLS wholesale price index) or to increases in the pipeline's regulated selling prices (which are partly determined by the cost of field gas, hence the term "spiral").[33]

In an attempt to enforce the price ceilings imposed in 1960, the FPC ruled that indefinite pricing clauses (except five-year redetermination clauses, which were subject to commission approval) would not be accepted in contracts executed on or after April 3, 1961.[34]

---

[32] Garfield and Lovejoy, *Public Utility Economics*, p. 319. The average wellhead value of gas declined from 11.1¢/Mcf in 1922 to a low of 4.5¢/Mcf in 1940.

[33] Neuner, *Natural Gas Industry*, p. 84.

[34] 25 FPC 379, 609 (1961), 27 FPC 339 (1962); upheld by the Supreme Court Permian Basin Area Rate Cases, 390 U.S. 747 (1968), pp. 781-784.

Since escalator clauses in old contracts were triggered by new contract prices and since new contract prices were now frozen, this ruling had the effect of making existing indefinite escalator clauses inoperative. It eliminated the producer's protection against inflation and his automatic gain from improved market conditions. The only way the producer's field price of gas could now rise was by FPC action.

Another variety of contract provision, the "take-or-pay clause," has been used to avoid the commission's price controls. Under this provision, the buyer of gas agrees to pay for a certain amount of gas each year whether or not the gas is actually taken. If the buyer does not take the gas during some specified future period, the payment is forfeited. In addition to assuring the producer of a minimum annual income from each contract, the take-or-pay provision offers an obvious way to circumvent the FPC's ceiling rates by letting the producer earn interest on income derived from earlier payment. The commission attempted to deal with this problem by specifying that no contract executed after February 1, 1967, would be accepted unless it permitted a minimum five-year makeup period for pipelines to take gas for which prepayments had been made under take-or-pay provisions.[35]

---

[35] 37 FPC 110.

2

HISTORY AND PURPOSE
OF FIELD PRICE REGULATION

As noted, the Federal Power Commission regulates the natural gas industry under the authority granted it by the Natural Gas Act of 1938.[1] The history of regulation of the field market under this act can be divided into four periods: (1) the period of no controls, 1938-54; (2) the period of individual producer regulation, 1954-60; (3) the period of area rate regulation, 1960-68;[2] and (4) the period of shortage, approximately 1968 to the present. Each of these periods is discussed briefly below.

The Period of No Controls, 1938-54

From the passage of the Natural Gas Act in 1938 until the *Phillips* decision in 1954,[3] the FPC made no attempt to regulate sales of natural gas by independent producers to interstate pipelines. The Natural Gas Act contained the statement, "The provisions of this act . . . shall not apply . . . to the production or gathering of natural gas,"[4] and this exemption led the FPC to deny it had any jurisdiction over producer sales in the field. Given this exemption some observers find it baffling that the Supreme Court ruled in 1954

---

[1] 15 U.S.C. 717. This act was similar to the Federal Power Act of 1935. Both granted the FPC jurisdiction over interstate sales—the 1935 act over sales of electricity and the 1938 act over sales of natural gas (a power previously denied to state regulatory agencies by the Supreme Court). See Missouri v. Kansas Natural Gas Co., 265 U.S. 298 (1924).

[2] Since area rate regulation was in effect until 1974, this is an arbitrary dividing line chosen to indicate the FPC's change in policy designed to stimulate the search for new domestic supplies.

[3] Phillips Petroleum Co. v. Wisconsin, 347 U.S. 672 (1954).

[4] 15 U.S.C. 717 (b) (1964).

that the FPC had a legal responsibility to regulate field market prices. Yet, as Kitch points out, the 1954 *Phillips* decision had a "certain perverse historical correctness" about it.[5] The act of 1938 was passed to prevent higher consumer prices caused by a natural gas shortage. Regulation of pipelines alone does not prevent higher field prices from being passed on to consumers.[6] Also, while the act clearly applied to "sales for resale" in interstate commerce, it was ambiguous in determining at what point the gas produced and gathered by independent producers came under the FPC's jurisdiction.

The Supreme Court's decision in *Phillips* extended to independent producers the line of reasoning used in a series of cases involving the FPC's jurisdiction over gas produced by interstate pipelines.[7] In this series, the Court established that the exemption of "production and gathering" did not apply to gas produced by pipeline companies and that the FPC should use some form of rate-base regulation to regulate pipeline-produced gas. This meant that the commission must attempt to include the estimated value of the producing property in each company's rate base and devise a rate schedule yielding a specified rate of return on the rate base.

The *Phillips* case involved an independent producer of natural gas that did not operate interstate pipelines. When Phillips Petroleum Company, the largest independent producer, raised its prices for interstate gas, it was challenged before the FPC by Wisconsin and the cities of Milwaukee, Kansas City, and Detroit. The commission stated that it did not have jurisdiction over transportation or sales made in the production or gathering of natural gas.[8] The FPC's decision was appealed to the courts and was reversed first by the D.C. Court of Appeals[9] and later by the Supreme Court. The Supreme Court relied on the distinction it had established in 1947 between "production and gathering of natural gas" and "sales of such gas in interstate commerce."[10]

---

[5] Kitch, "Regulation of Field Market," p. 255.

[6] Ibid., pp. 255-256.

[7] The most important of these were Colorado Interstate Gas Co. v. FPC and Canadian River Gas Co. v. FPC, 324 U.S. 581 (1945); Interstate Natural Gas Co. v. FPC, 331 U.S. 682 (1947); FPC v. Panhandle Eastern Pipeline Company, 337 U.S. 498 (1949); 230 F.2d 810 (1955); 352 U.S. 891.

[8] 10 FPC 246 (1951).

[9] 205 F.2d 706.

[10] Interstate Natural Gas Co. v. FPC, 331 U.S. 682, 692-693 (1947).

The Period of Independent Producer Regulation, 1954-60

Faced with its new responsibility, the Federal Power Commission tackled the problem of regulating the field (or producer) market. After consultation with the industry, it decided to extend to individual producers the rate-of-return/rate-base regulation used for pipelines. For several reasons, this approach did not reduce field prices during this period (see Figure 1)—although prices for new gas fell from 1958 on because of declining demand. First, the FPC was slow to begin individual cost-of-service regulation because it expected Congress to amend the Natural Gas Act to exclude authority over independent producers. An amendment to this effect, the Harris-Fulbright bill, was passed by Congress in 1956 but was vetoed by President Eisenhower, who supported the principles of the bill but objected to the "arrogant lobbying" for its passage.[11] Other attempts were made to amend the Natural Gas Act, but no bills reached the floor of Congress, primarily because of continuing lobbying scandals. Professor Edith Carter concludes her analysis of the lobbying as follows:

> After 1958 the conflict shifted from Congress back to the regulatory arena. The basic position of the FPC, which favored exempting producers, remained unchanged. However, since Congress had failed to amend the Natural Gas Act, the Commission turned to the problem of finding a formula for producer regulation as decreed by the Supreme Court in the Phillips decision in 1954.[12]

Second, the FPC did not have the work force to act on the large volume of rate schedules and supplements submitted by producers. Before the 1954 *Phillips* decision, the commission averaged about 100 certificate applications and 700 gas-rate filings each year. In the first year after *Phillips*, this increased to 6,047 producer certificate applications and about 11,000 producer rate schedules. By 1960, the commission had more than 33,000 supplements to rate schedules on file.[13] A substantial backlog developed.

Third, the common result of those pre-1960 cases decided on a cost-of-service basis was approval of the requested rate increases. In ten out of eleven cost-of-service cases decided by the FPC during the period 1955-60, the method of computing costs more than justi-

---

[11] Carter, *Lobbying and the Natural Gas Bill*, p. 36.

[12] Ibid., p. 39.

[13] Garfield and Lovejoy, *Public Utility Economics*, p. 330.

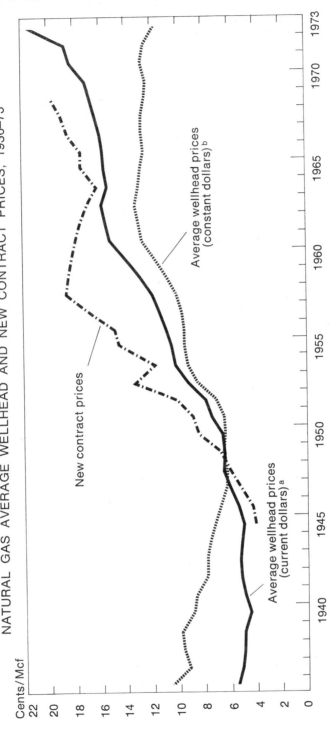

Figure 1

NATURAL GAS AVERAGE WELLHEAD AND NEW CONTRACT PRICES, 1936–73

a Average wellhead price for 1973 is a Bureau of Mines preliminary estimate.
b 1947–49 = 100.

Source: Average wellhead prices from U.S. Bureau of Mines, *Minerals Yearbook*, 1936–72. Weighted-average new contract prices for the seven southwest producing states from Foster Associates, Inc.

fied the proposed prices. The remaining case could not be resolved. In addition, the five cases involving pipeline-produced gas which were decided on a cost-of-service basis showed unit costs higher than market rates.[14]

Fourth, those cases decided on the basis of "fair market value" could not be expected to affect prices much since the standard for approving a field price was the decision that the price had been "competitively" determined in that market area.

To say that FPC regulation was ineffective in reducing field prices up to 1960 is not to say that the regulation failed to impose costs on the producers of natural gas. Robert W. Gerwig has estimated that the costs imposed came to approximately 7 percent of the base price of natural gas in the Gulf Coast market during the years 1956 to 1958. The total cost to the industry was estimated to be about $84 million per year.[15] By comparing interstate and intrastate prices, Gerwig has concluded that producers considered this cost of regulation in negotiating their prices with interstate pipelines.

The FPC was under increased political pressure because of increased prices for gas. Figure 1 shows the average cost of all field purchases for the years 1936-73 and new contract prices for the years 1945-69. As noted before, the postwar period of rapid expansion in the pipeline system greatly increased the demand for new gas in the producing areas. This, along with the operation of various renegotiation clauses, increased the cost of yearly gas purchases. For the ten year period 1948-58, average wellhead prices increased 83 percent (6.5 to 11.9¢/Mcf)[16] and new contract prices increased 210 percent (from 6 to 18.6¢/Mcf).[17]

The postwar period of rising prices followed the long period during the 1920s and 1930s when there were declining or stable prices. This led many observers (including the Supreme Court in its 1959 CATCO decision)[18] to conclude that the FPC should do some-

---

[14] Ibid., p. 346.

[15] Robert W. Gerwig, "Natural Gas Production: A Study of Costs of Regulation," *Journal of Law and Economics*, vol. 5 (October 1962), p. 85.

[16] Bureau of Mines, *Minerals Yearbook*, various years.

[17] Data are weighted average new contract prices for seven southwest states compiled by Foster Associates, Inc. from forms filed with the FPC by natural gas producers. This series was presented as Schedule 1, Exhibit No. 24 in Docket No. AR69-1. The new contract prices were weighted by the quantities of gas extracted during the first year of each contract.

[18] Atlantic Refining Company v. Public Service Commission, 360 U.S. 378 (1959), commonly called the CATCO decision.

thing "to afford consumers a complete . . . bond of protection from excessive rates and charges."[19] The political pressure along with the extreme administrative difficulties facing the commission[20] led the FPC to set out its problems with individual cost-of-service regulation in the second *Phillips* case in 1960.[21] The difficulties discussed in this case became the basis for establishing area rate regulation later that year.[22]

The Period of Area Rate Regulation, 1960-68

The basic procedure in area rate regulation was the establishment of a maximum price for gas based on the average cost of production in each of the producing areas in the country. Hearings were conducted for each area to establish "just and reasonable" rates. Until the hearings could be finished, the commission froze prices by refusing to approve initial contract rates higher than the previous high rate approved for each area and to grant price increases for old contracts which had prices above the average for each area.[23] This price freeze established what has been called the "in line" pricing doctrine. The doctrine was based on the view that the way to protect consumers was to keep current prices "in line" with past prices.[24]

Area rate regulation reduced the FPC's administrative burden. The commission now had to consider in detail only those interstate contracts above the price ceilings set in each area.[25] Its major effort during most of this period was devoted to its first area rate hearings for the Permian Basin, the large producing area in southeast New Mexico and west Texas. The initial order announcing the Permian area rate hearing was issued in December 1960. Preliminary hearings were held in the Permian area in March 1961, with formal

---

[19] Ibid., at 388.

[20] For a recent discussion of these problems, see Stephen Breyer and Paul W. MacAvoy, "The Natural Gas Shortage and the Regulation of Natural Gas Producers," *Harvard Law Review*, vol. 86, no. 6 (April 1973), pp. 952-958.

[21] Phillips Petroleum Co., 24 FPC 537 (1960) at 542-548. Wisconsin v. FPC, 373 U.S. 294 (1963).

[22] Statement of General Policy No. 61-1, 24 FPC 818 (September 1960).

[23] Ibid.

[24] This doctrine was originally espoused by the Supreme Court in the CATCO decision, 360 U.S. 378. For a discussion of the CATCO decision, see Kitch, "Field Market for Natural Gas," pp. 260-265.

[25] There are other reasons why this task was made easier. See the discussion below, pp. 33-41.

hearings beginning in Washington in October 1961. After four and one-half years of hearings, the final FPC opinion was issued in August 1965,[26] and three years later the Supreme Court gave its final approval.[27] This long period of price controls coupled with producer uncertainty about the prices which would eventually be allowed by the FPC must have dampened producers' expectations and restricted decisions for exploration and development of natural gas.

The FPC opinion announced in August 1965 established an area rate ceiling for new gas in the Permian Basin that was 3.2 percent below the ceiling rate established for that area in 1960.[28] This lower price, along with the commission's even lower ceiling for old gas sold under contracts dated before January 1, 1961, indicated to producers that the FPC was establishing stringent price controls.

The Permian "two tier" system—a lower price for old gas than for new—has remained an integral part of FPC policy in all area rate cases. Further, it is now appearing in a slightly different form in current proposals which call for deregulation of new gas only. The purpose of setting a lower ceiling for "old" gas already committed to the interstate market is to transfer income from producers to consumers.[29] The reasoning is that gas already under contract is fixed in supply so that controlling its price will not affect the quantity of gas delivered to pipelines and ultimately to consumers. If demand increases and consumers become willing to pay higher prices for gas, the price controls on old gas will prevent field producers from realizing a windfall profit. Only new gas will require a higher price as an incentive to bring the gas to the interstate market.

The principal difficulty with this argument is that it assumes that producers do not learn from experience. If the FPC continually redefines committed gas as "old gas" by moving the cutoff date between old and new gas forward in time, producers will

---

[26] Joe L. Steele, *The Use of Econometric Models by Federal Regulatory Agencies* (Lexington, Mass.: Heath Lexington Books, 1971), p. 10. For another extensive study of the Permian hearing and opinion, see Hawkins, *Field Price Regulation*. The FPC's Permian Basin decision was Opinion No. 468, 34 FPC 159 (1965).

[27] Permian Basin Area Rate Cases, 390 U.S. 747 (1968).

[28] J. Daniel Khazzoom, *An Econometric Model of U.S. Natural Gas Supply*, Docket No. AR69-1, Southern Louisiana Area Rate Proceedings (Washington, D. C.: Federal Power Commission, Office of Economics, September 1970), Table A-4.

[29] See the discussion of this in Breyer and MacAvoy, "The Natural Gas Shortage," pp. 949-952, 959-965, 984-985; and Hawkins, "Natural Gas Producing Industry," pp. 161-163.

quickly learn that the initial price they negotiate for an interstate contract will remain fixed over the life of the contract.[30] Under this policy the total annual revenues allowed by the FPC can be accurately predicted. The producer can compare this expected stream of future receipts with his expected future costs to make his decision about searching for and developing new gas reserves for the interstate market. With smaller amounts of new gas being discovered, gas discovered in previous years becomes more important in contract negotiations. This means that the producers' anticipation of the FPC price-freezing policy for "old" gas increases in importance first in the development process and later in the exploration process. Since the "two tier" policy has now been carried out by the FPC for thirteen years,[31] it is likely that producers have almost all anticipated the FPC's price freeze even in their initial decisions about exploring for new reserves.[32]

This anticipation of the price freeze should have several predictable consequences. First, when producers compare the stream of future receipts allowed by the FPC with the expected stream of future costs, only those producers who expect low costs will have an incentive to search for gas and to commit it to the interstate market. This means that exploratory drilling in high cost areas will be strongly affected.[33] Second, as producers anticipate new inflation, their expected future costs increase. This reduces their estimate of the present value of any reserves discovered and committed to the interstate market.[34] As producers anticipate new inflation, they will (1) be disinclined to search for or develop new gas, (2) seek short-term contracts which promise quick payment, and (3) avoid the interstate market in favor of the unregulated intra-

---

[30] The FPC does allow some fixed escalation clauses, typically 1¢ every four years.

[31] Since the announcement of area rate regulation and the "in-line" pricing policy in 1960; 24 FPC 818 (1960).

[32] For a discussion of anticipated inflation, see Reuben A. Kessel and Armen A. Alchian, "The Effects of Inflation," *Journal of Political Economy,* vol. 70 (December 1962), pp. 521-537.

[33] Given the uncertainty (that is, variability of cost) inherent in exploratory drilling, some drilling will take place in anticipation of finding a low-cost source. If instead gas is discovered which appears to be expensive to develop and market, the field may not be developed.

[34] Present value may be defined as the sum of the discounted stream of net revenue where each year's net receipts are discounted by the market rate of interest. If the market rate of interest includes an allowance for inflation, future net receipts will be discounted more heavily the greater the expected inflation.

state market. With the annual increase in the wholesale price index averaging 4.8 percent since 1965, producers' anticipation of cost inflation must have had a strong influence on decisions about exploration, development, and interstate sales.[35] If the rate of inflation continues to increase, the consequences of anticipated inflation can be expected to be felt even more strongly.

A third consequence of the "two tier" system of price control is that the equilibrium (nonregulated) price for new gas will be higher than it would be in the absence of price controls on old contracts. As the producer learns that his original negotiated price may be expected to continue for the life of the contract, he will increase his estimate of a minimum acceptable price. Thus, if the area rate ceiling is binding for new gas (that is, if it is less than the equilibrium price), any resulting shortage will be larger than in the absence of the separate (and lower) ceiling on old contracts.

The result is that, over time, as producers anticipate the FPC's policy, less gas is made available to the interstate gas consumer. The consumer ends up paying more and getting less gas than he would in the absence of the "two tier" system.[36] The FPC's "two tier" system probably resulted in a sizeable transfer of wealth in the early 1960s when the policy was new and a large proportion of gas was found jointly with oil, but the ability to continue such a transfer in the 1970s will be slight.

The Period of Shortage, 1968 to the Present

By September 1968, the FPC had issued its southern Louisiana area rate decision and the proceedings in the Hugoton-Anadarko and Texas Gulf Coast areas were well under way. The commission was slowly becoming aware of a looming shortage of natural gas. In fact, 1968 was the first year the American Gas Association (AGA) reserve data showed annual consumption to be larger than additions to reserves. The declining reserves-to-production ratio (R/P) along

---

[35] Unless it can somehow be shown that the set of businessmen known as natural gas producers somehow learn about the effects of inflation at a slower rate than other businessmen or consumers.

[36] This same argument has been made repeatedly in the literature on inflation and economic development where it is argued that a government may transfer real purchasing power from consumers to itself by inflating its currency at a faster rate than the population anticipates. Obviously, the payoff of such a scheme grows increasingly smaller as consumers anticipate inflation and take appropriate action (that is, raise the prices of goods they sell to the government) to protect themselves.

with the commission's own estimates of growing demand led the commission to mention in its 1969 annual report that the "effect of area price regulation on gas supplies for interstate deliveries" was under review.[37] By 1971 the FPC had gone to great lengths to document the shortage situation brought about by declining exploratory drilling and growing demand.[38]

The growing shortage of natural gas has led to a substantial change in FPC policy since 1968. Some of the major actions taken by the commission to stimulate exploration and dedication of reserves to the interstate market are noted here.

(1) The commission has raised area ceiling prices in most areas. For example, ceiling rates in south Louisiana were raised 40.5 percent (to 26¢/Mcf), in the Texas Gulf Coast 41 percent (to 24¢), in Kansas 18.8 percent (to 19¢), in Oklahoma 33.3 percent (to 20¢), and in Permian Basin 112 percent (to 35¢).

(2) The commission has offered special incentives in south Louisiana and the Gulf Coast to producers dedicating gas to the interstate market. These include the tying of future price escalations to the attainment of industry-wide interstate dedication goals and the forgiving of previously ordered refund obligations in proportion to interstate dedications.

(3) The commission has allowed regulated pipelines to include research and development costs and advance payments to producers for exploration and development in the cost of service to be covered by the rate-making process.

(4) The commission has exempted small producers from certain filing and certification regulations.

(5) The commission has allowed pipelines to make "emergency" purchases of gas on a short-term basis at rates higher than area rates.

(6) The commission has speeded up the regulatory process by adopting a rulemaking procedure in the place of the previous adversary proceeding.[39]

(7) The commission has adopted a new "optional pricing" procedure whereby pipelines with a critical supply situation can purchase new gas reserves under long-term contracts at rates negotiated between buyer and seller. An important provision of "optional

---

[37] FPC, *Annual Report, 1969*, p. 45.

[38] FPC, *Annual Report, 1971*, pp. 31-36.

[39] All of the above are summarized, along with some other minor points, in FPC, *Annual Report, 1971*, pp. 36-46. The Permian Basin data (35¢/Mcf) is from *FPC News*, August 10, 1973, p. 4.

pricing" is that the commission cannot later change the negotiated contract price. This is an attempt to reduce producer uncertainty about what will actually be paid for future interstate gas sales.[40]

(8) The most successful FPC policy for persuading producers to sell gas to the interstate market has been the issuance of "limited term certificates." This policy allows producers to commit gas to the interstate market for short periods of time at rates higher than the area rates set by the commission. Of the 1.1 Tcf of gas dedicated to the interstate market in 1973, 31 percent (340 Bcf) was obtained by this procedure.[41]

In its most recent move the FPC has eliminated its limited term and emergency-sales procedures and replaced individual area price ceilings with a single nationwide ceiling of 42¢/Mcf.[42] A separate single rate for old gas is to be announced within a few months, with the dividing line between old and new gas being January 1, 1973. While the new ceiling is above the old area rate ceilings, it is still substantially below the intrastate prices paid for most unregulated gas.

It seems that the purpose of regulation has changed from protecting consumers from higher prices to protecting consumers from natural gas shortages by allowing higher prices.

---

[40] FPC, *Optional Procedure for Certificating New Producer Sales of Natural Gas*, Docket No. R-441, Order No. 455, issued August 3, 1972. For opposition to this procedure see "Gas Price Policy of FPC Worries Key Congressmen," *Wall Street Journal*, November 13, 1972. Optional pricing is now under court attack by Congressman Moss in John E. Moss et al. v. FPC.

[41] James G. Phillips, "Energy Report/Congress Nears Showdown on Proposal to Decontrol Gas Prices," *National Journal Reports*, May 25, 1974, p. 765.

[42] *Wall Street Journal*, June 24, 1974, p. 4. The new policy also provides for 1¢/year escalation and some allowances for taxes and gathering costs. This policy was originally proposed by the FPC in Docket No. R-389B, April 11, 1973.

3

THE ECONOMICS OF AN
UNREGULATED GAS MARKET

The fact that the FPC was not able to establish effective controls on field prices until September 1960 makes it possible for the postwar history of the natural gas market to be divided into two distinct periods—a period of no regulation (1945-60) and a period of regulation (1961 to the present). With this time division, the effects of field market regulation can be studied by comparing producers' responses to important economic forces before and after price controls were established. This procedure assumes that if price controls had not been instituted, producers would have continued to respond to important economic forces during the 1960s as they had done during the period 1945-60.[1]

The procedure employed in this study involves using multiple regression techniques to estimate the relationship between certain natural gas output (dependent) variables and other (independent) variables representing the important economic forces affecting producers' decisions. The model and regression results are presented in Appendix A. What follows here is a discussion of the basic ideas behind the model.

Procedure for Estimating Unregulated Industry Behavior

If, for some reason, the price offered producers for new gas in long-term gas contracts increased, then the producers could profitably develop and sell larger quantities of new gas. The incentive provided by higher prices and profits would cause producers (1) to commit larger amounts of already discovered gas to long-term con-

---

[1] This basic procedure has also been used by Khazzoom, Erickson and Spann, and MacAvoy in their studies of natural gas regulation.

tracts, (2) to increase the rate of development drilling in fields which have already been discovered, and (3) to increase the intensity of the search for new gas fields. A decrease in the price offered on long-term contracts could be expected to have the opposite effects. Since it takes several years to develop a new gas field, we know that the effect of a given price change will be spread out over several years. Adelman has argued that an assumption of three years is not unreasonable, although it may take anywhere from one to six years to develop a typical field.[2] Because the adjustment to a price change in one year will usually not be completed that year, the model deemed most appropriate for estimating the supply response of natural gas producers is a distributed-lag model.

A distributed-lag model uses the idea of a "desired" stock of reserves. In this model, the stock of reserves which producers would like to have at the end of the year is assumed to be a function of three petroleum prices—the initial price of gas for long-term contracts, the price of crude oil, and the price of natural gas liquids. These three variables are selected to represent the "important economic forces" affecting producers' decisions.

The new contract price of gas is included because it is probably the best available indicator of the price the producer can expect to receive for his gas in the future. It is expected that the estimating procedure will find new contract prices to be positively correlated with the desired stock of gas reserves.

The prices of crude oil and natural gas liquids are included because of the joint nature of the search for these two products and for natural gas. Natural gas and natural gas liquids are produced together. Therefore, an increase in the price of liquids would be expected to increase the value of natural gas reserves and encourage producers to intensify their search for natural gas. The effect of an increase in the price of crude oil depends upon the extent to which "directionality" exists in the search for natural gas.[3] The degree of directionality in petroleum drilling refers to the extent producers can change the odds of finding oil or gas by selecting different types

[2] M. A. Adelman, "Trends in Cost of Finding and Developing Oil and Gas in the U.S.," in Essays in Petroleum Economics, ed. Steve H. Hanke and Stephen L. Gardner (Golden, Colo.: Colorado School of Mines, 1967), p. 70.

[3] For discussions of the topic of directionality in drilling, see J. Daniel Khazzoom, "Gas Directionality," Public Utilities Fortnightly, vol. 84 (December 18, 1969), pp. 20-25; and Erickson and Spann, "Supply Response in a Regulated Industry: The Case of Natural Gas," The Bell Journal of Economics and Management Science, vol. 2, no. 1 (Spring 1971), pp. 96-101 and p. 107, especially footnote 29.

of geological formations for drilling. If the price of oil rises relative to the price of gas and directionality is strong, then producers will be more inclined to drill in geological formations in which the probability of finding oil is greater and less inclined to drill in likely gas producing formations. On the other hand, if directionality is weak, producers will not respond to changes in oil and gas prices by changing the type of formations drilled. The historical version of the weak directionality argument held that producers drilled only for oil and that gas was found only as a by-product of oil search.[4] Assuming that there is relatively strong directionality in the oil and gas search, a negative or inverse relationship can be predicted between crude oil prices and natural gas discoveries. But this effect may be difficult to measure in the absence of large relative changes in the prices of oil and gas.

With the desired level of reserves determined by the gas, oil, and liquids prices, the distributed-lag model estimates the "usual" or "average" adjustment made by producers to close any discrepancy between the desired level of reserves in a particular year (t) and the actual level of reserves at the end of the previous year (t-1). After estimating the relationship between the dependent output variable (natural gas reserves or additions to reserves or new discoveries) and each of the independent explanatory variables for the preregulation period (1945-60), one can use the estimated coefficients to project the output variable for the period or regulation (1961-69) under the assumption that producers, had there been no regulation, would have responded to economic forces in the same way they did when there was no regulation. In the projection procedure, actual crude oil and natural gas liquid prices were used as exogenous data. The projections of the output variables were made on a year-to-year basis so as to take advantage of the estimate of "usual" adjustment by the industry from one year to the next.

Since area-rate regulation may have influenced new contract prices in the 1960s, the actual new contract prices could not be used in the projection procedure. Therefore a series of "unregulated" prices were estimated for the 1960s, based on a reduced-form model containing one demand variable and two supply variables.[5]

---

[4] Note that this last argument implies that regulation of gas prices would have little effect on the supply of gas. This argument was a product of the pre-World War II gas market when, before the development of an extensive pipeline system, the value of gas was low relative to the value of oil in the Southwest. However, even after conditions changed, this same line of reasoning was used to justify price controls in the 1960s.

[5] See the appendix for the details of this procedure.

The demand variable attempted to allow for the growth of gas markets, a major influence on field market prices. Using these "unregulated" prices to estimate what natural gas reserves would have been in the 1960s, we should get a series of estimates of how the industry would have responded had the FPC not been required to impose price controls.

The AGA and AAPG Data

The following accounting identity summarizes the way the American Gas Association (AGA) collects and publishes its data on natural gas reserves:[6]

$$R_{t-1} + ND_t + XR_t - QF_t + S_t \equiv R_t.$$

R_t is the level (stock) of proven reserves at the end of year t, ND_t is new discoveries of gas during year t, XR_t is extensions and revisions to reserves during the year, QF_t is the quantity of field gas produced (extracted) during the year, and S_t is the net change in underground storage. Extensions to reserves can be considered the best available indicator of the output of development drilling and new discoveries the best available indicator of the output of the exploration process.[7] Revisions to reserves include modifications of past estimates and corrections of past mistakes. Revisions probably contain large random components not influenced in any known way by natural gas producers.

With this breakdown of AGA data, it is possible to make projections in three different ways. The first uses the level of proven reserves (R_t) as the dependent variable. It is the most straightforward application of the distributed-lag model. The second isolates the data on additions to reserves ($NDXR$, new discoveries plus extensions plus revisions) as the dependent output variable under the assumption that these exploration and development data represent a close approximation to producers' response to economic stimuli.[8] An additional refinement to the model is the use of new

---

[6] AGA, *Reserves of Crude Oil, Natural Gas Liquids and Natural Gas in the United States and Canada*, various years. This is a joint publication of the American Gas Association (AGA), the American Petroleum Institute (API), and the Canadian Petroleum Association. It is henceforth referred to as *Reserves*.

[7] Adelman, "Trends in Cost," p. 70.

[8] This refinement includes data for revisions which do not respond to economic forces in any known way. Data on revisions have been published separately from extensions only since 1966.

discoveries only (ND) as the dependent variable. This eliminates the erratic data contained in revisions.

As a check, a fourth dependent variable derived from a different source—the American Association of Petroleum Geologists' (AAPG) data on successful exploratory footage drilled for gas—is used. This variable is adopted as an additional proxy variable to measure producers' response to economic conditions.[9]

Results

The evidence on the effect of FPC regulation on field prices is presented in Figure 2 and in Appendix Table A-1. These compare actual new contract prices with the prices predicted by the reduced-form model. The model shows an upward trend in prices until 1963, a decline in prices from 1963 to 1967, and then a fairly sharp increase in prices after 1967. The decline in prices from 1963 to 1967 is consistent with Kitch's argument that the demand for new field gas declined during this period while supplies of new gas were still increasing. The decline in demand resulted from a decline in the rate of growth of pipelines and from increased competition from coal and electricity. The increase in supply was the result of the unusually large quantities of gas found by extensive development drilling of previously discovered reserves.[10]

This "unregulated" price pattern leads to the conclusion that the FPC's price freeze did keep average new contract prices below the levels they would have reached in the absence of regulation. But the influence of the commission's policy varied greatly during the decade. This leads to a second conclusion. The strongest retardation of prices occurred before 1963 and after 1967, the period after 1967 being the most restrictive. The interim period 1963-67 was characterized by downward pressure on new contract prices as a result of large discoveries and the declining rate of growth in pipeline resale markets.

With a large proportion of new interstate gas contracts being negotiated at prices below the FPC's area ceiling rates in the middle 1960s, the administrative load on the commission fell, and the commission was enabled to concentrate on its *Permian Basin* case. It was, as noted, the commission's policy to review only those initial

---

[9] For the actual data and computation procedure see Robert B. Helms, *The Effectiveness of Federal Power Commission Regulation of the Field Market for Natural Gas* (Ph.D. diss., U.C.L.A., 1973), pp. 74-77, 179.

[10] Kitch, "Field Market for Natural Gas," pp. 265-269.

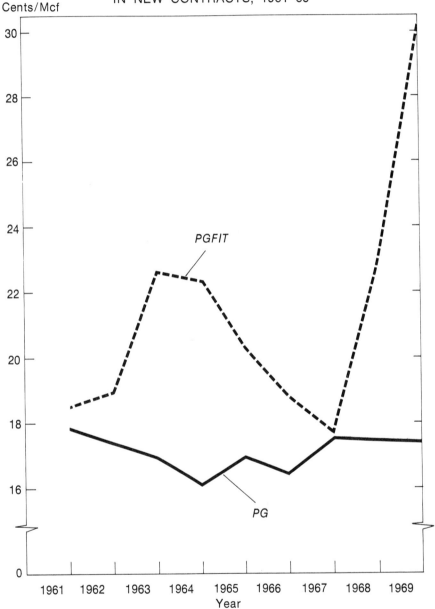

Figure 2

ACTUAL AND PROJECTED PRICES OF GAS
IN NEW CONTRACTS, 1961–69

PG = actual average price of gas in new contracts in seven southwest states.
PGFIT = projected average price of gas in new contracts with no regulation.

Source: Appendix Table A-1.

34

contract rates that were above the area rates—that is, only those contracts whose prices formed the upper part of the distribution of prices within an area. In many of these cases the commission disallowed the high rates or approved the contracts subject to refund. From the FPC's point of view, this was a vast improvement over the administrative task imposed in the 1950s by the original *Phillips* decision.[11] It gave the illusion that area regulation was a successful means by which to regulate the field market.

By 1968, when the Supreme Court completed its long judicial review of the *Permian Basin* decision, the illusion was beginning to be dispelled. The reduced-form model shows that new contract prices would have increased by 71 percent from 1967 to 1969. During this period actual new contract prices (as deflated by the wholesale price index) remained almost constant.[12] The commission's price controls therefore restricted price increases by approximately 13¢/Mcf.[13]

The effect of FPC regulation on search and on actual discovery is presented in Figures 3, 4, and 5 (and in Appendix Tables A-3 and A-4) which compare actual and projected data for total additions to reserves (NDXR), new discoveries (ND), and cumulative exploratory drilling footage (F).

The projections for $\hat{F}$ suggest a steadily increasing effect on the stock of exploratory footage drilled for gas. The rate of change of $\hat{F}$ is almost constant. The actual stock of exploratory footage (F) increased at a slower rate, and its rate of change was more erratic than the projected series. By 1969 the distributed lag model shows cumulative exploratory gas well footage 19 percent greater than the actual footage. The changes in the two stock series from 1968 to 1969 suggest that, in the absence of regulation, annual exploratory footage would have been approximately 47 million feet in 1969 as opposed to an actual figure of only 20.9 million feet. To the extent that this computation of exploratory footage can be taken as proxy for "search effort," the model indicates that the search for new gas reserves in 1969 was less than half as great as it might have been

---

[11] See the repeated discussions of the commission's attempts to reduce its backlog of cases in its annual reports from 1955 to 1962 and its reasons for establishing area rates in Phillips Petroleum Co., 24 FPC 537, 545-546 (1960).

[12] The deflated prices (1957-59 = 100) in 1967 and 1969 were 17.53 and 17.43 respectively while the corresponding nondeflated values were 18.6 and 19.7¢/Mcf.

[13] In 1969, the new contract prices filed with the FPC exceeded the area ceiling rates in twelve of the eighteen pricing areas where comparisons can be made.

Figure 3

CUMULATIVE ACTUAL AND PROJECTED EXPLORATORY GAS WELL FOOTAGE, 1961–69

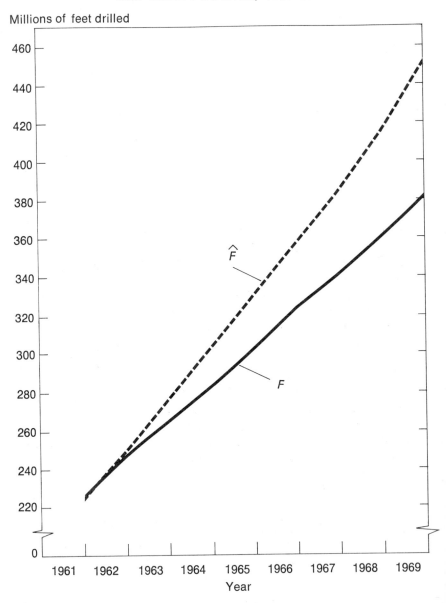

$\widehat{F}$ = estimated cumulative successful gas footage in the absence of FPC regulation.

F = actual cumulative successful gas footage.

Source: Appendix Table A-4.

Figure 4

ACTUAL AND PROJECTED NEW GAS DISCOVERIES PLUS
EXTENSIONS AND REVISIONS, 1961–69

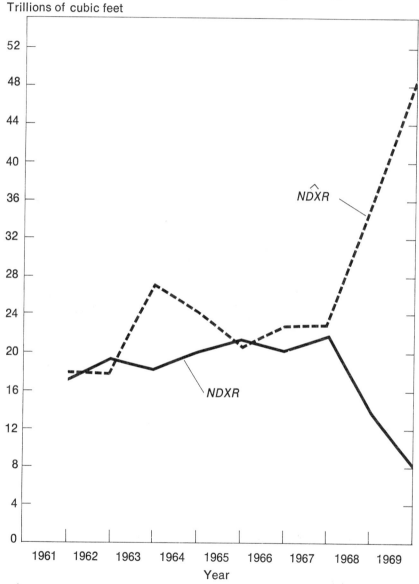

Trillions of cubic feet

Year

$\widehat{NDXR}$ = estimated new discoveries, extensions and revisions without FPC price controls.

$NDXR$ = actual new discoveries, extensions and revisions.

Source: Appendix Table A-3.

Figure 5

ACTUAL AND PROJECTED NEW GAS DISCOVERIES, 1961–69

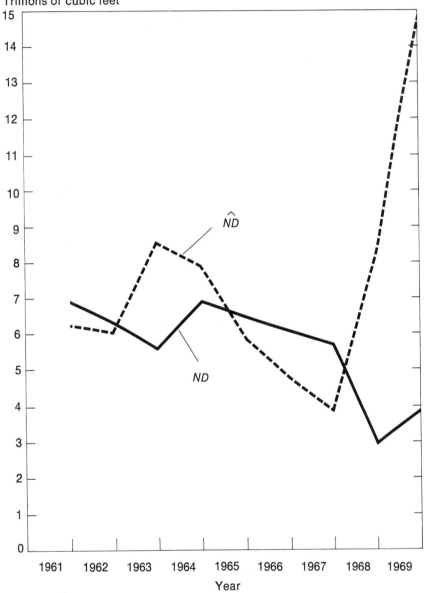

Trillions of cubic feet

$\widehat{ND}$ = estimated new discoveries of gas without FPC price controls.

ND = actual new discoveries.

Source: Appendix Table A-3.

if producers had been motivated by market-determined petroleum prices during the 1960s.

From the projections for the two categories of additions to reserves, $\hat{ND}$ and $\hat{NDXR}$, it can be seen that additions to reserves would have followed a pattern similar to $PGFIT$—declining from 1963 to about 1967 and then increasing in response to higher gas prices. As noted before, the year-to-year data on new discoveries should be more responsive to price changes than $NDXR$. This is the case with both the actual and predicted series. Even with actual ND declining, $NDXR$ continued to increase from 1963 to 1967 because of the increases in XR from the continuing development of already discovered fields. With the discovery of new fields declining from 1964 to 1968 the development process gradually became more complete.[14] This should account for the almost constant level of $NDXR$ from 1964 through 1967 and the decline after 1967.[15]

The most notable feature of the comparison between predicted and actual reserve additions is the lack of response of actual reserve additions to the upturn in gas prices in 1968 and 1969 even though ND was slightly larger in 1969 than in 1968. Both ND and XR responded to the decline in market prices before 1967, and the model shows this pattern would have been followed even in the absence of regulation. The conclusion must be that the FPC's area rate regulation did not have any detectable effect on the search for (and discovery of) natural gas until after 1967 when price controls became binding. If the uncertainties resulting from regulation also had a depressing effect on search and discoveries before 1967, this is not separable from the general effect of declining market prices. In any event, on the basis of the preregulation structural parameters, the model shows that the industry could have been expected substantially to increase discovery and development of new gas reserves after 1967 in the absence of price controls.

Figure 6 and Appendix Table A-3 presents the comparison between the actual and predicted stock of reserves. The model shows that without price control the stock of reserves ($\hat{R}$) would have increased until 1965 at a rate slightly greater than the actual rate of increase. This would have produced a stock of reserves approximately 3 percent greater than the actual stock at the end of

---

[14] This lag in XR relative to ND is consistent with the usual argument (discussed in Chapter 1) that the development of a new field is completed in approximately six years.

[15] Extensions to reserves from 1966 through 1972 were 9.2, 9.5, 7.8, 5.8, 6.2, 6.4, and 6.2 Tcf, indicating declining development drilling (AGA, *Reserves*).

Figure 6

ACTUAL AND PROJECTED GAS RESERVES, 1961–69

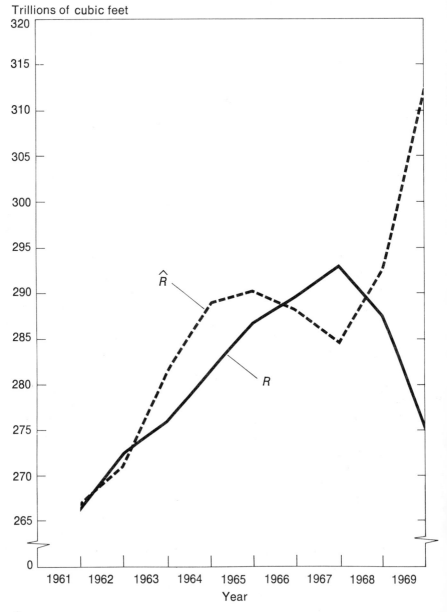

Trillions of cubic feet

$\widehat{R}$ = estimated stock of reserves without FPC regulation.
R = actual stock of reserves.

Source: Appendix Table A-3.

40

1964. From 1964 to 1967 the estimated stock of reserves without price controls declined (in response to the decline in *PGFIT*), but it increased in 1968 and 1969. During this period the actual stock of reserves continued its increase until 1968 when reserves declined for the first time since data became available. For 1969 the predicted stock of reserves without price controls was 14 percent greater than the actual stock, suggesting a reserves-to-production ratio of 15.1 instead of the 13.3 actually recorded.[16] This shortage of gas amounts to 37.7 trillion cubic feet, approximately twice the total domestic consumption in 1969.

The evidence suggests that the FPC's task of regulating field prices was eased considerably by the factors that would have led to a decline in market determined prices before about 1967. By the times prices should have increased, area rates were firmly established. After 1967, the FPC area rates helped prevent the industry from responding to higher market demand through increased exploration and development.

---

[16] FPC, *National Gas Supply and Demand*, Table 24, p. 139.

4
EVALUATION OF
FPC REGULATION

The conclusions reached in Chapter 3 can now be used to evaluate the achievement of field market regulation. The first goal of field market regulation is to fulfill the congressional and Supreme Court mandate to "assist the development of conditions which will lead to continuing and adequate supplies of natural gas at reasonable prices."[1] The second major goal is to stimulate additional domestic exploration for new supplies in order to meet the shortages which have been growing since about 1967.

A Policy for Providing Adequate
Supplies at Reasonable Prices

This study concludes that area rate regulation has not provided "continuing and adequate supplies." Rate regulation prevented prices from rising in response to growing demand and thereby prevented producers from responding to the higher demand. As a result, since 1967 there has been a declining reserve inventory, diversion of gas to the intrastate market, increasing curtailments of gas service, and increasing use of higher-cost alternative energy sources. Each of these effects is discussed below.

Natural gas reserve data come from two sources: the FPC's reports from regulated pipeline companies (Forms 15 and 15-A) and the AGA's estimates obtained from producers. Both sources clearly

---

[1] FPC, *Annual Report, 1969*, p. 43. See Edmund W. Kitch, "Regulation of Field Market," pp. 248-265, for a historical account of the development of this purpose.

indicate declining reserves for the forty-eight contiguous states.[2] The FPC's data on reserves owned or under contract by interstate pipelines show this most dramatically. They reflect both reduced exploration and the diversion of gas to the unregulated intrastate market. Table 2 shows interstate gas reserves and the amount of gas that pipelines added to their reserves, either from company exploration and development or (mostly) from contracts with independent producers. Total reserves peaked in 1967 and gross additions dropped off sharply after 1967. This indicates that the effect of regulation on interstate pipelines was even greater than the effect on total reserves (AGA data) that is estimated in the present study. This effect on the interstate pipelines is not surprising considering the amount of gas diverted to the unregulated intrastate market.

Table 2

INTERSTATE PIPELINE COMPANIES: TOTAL DOMESTIC RESERVES AND GROSS ADDITIONS TO RESERVES, 1963-72
(trillions of cubic feet)

Year	Pipeline Domestic Reserves	Total Domestic Pipeline Production	Domestic Reserves ÷ Production	Gross Additions	Gross Additions ÷ Production
1963	188.5	9.4	20.1	—	—
1964	189.2	10.0	18.9	10.6	1.06
1965	192.1	10.4	18.5	13.3	1.28
1966	195.1	11.1	17.5	14.2	1.27
1967	198.1	11.8	16.8	14.8	1.25
1968	195.0	12.6	15.5	9.5	.75
1969	187.6	13.4	14.0	6.1	.45
1970	173.6	14.1	12.3	0.04	.003
1971	161.4	14.2	11.5	1.9	.134
1972	146.9	14.2	10.3	− 0.24	− .017

Source: FPC, *The Gas Supplies of Interstate Natural Gas Pipeline Companies, 1972* (Washington, D. C.: Federal Power Commission, May 1974), pp. 2-9. Gross additions are the total of revisions to pipeline-owned or contracted reserves plus new additions.

[2] Of the 37.2 Tcf recorded as additions to reserves (NDXR) in 1970, 26.0 Tcf were from the new Prudhoe Bay Field on the North Slope of Alaska (FPC, *National Gas Supply and Demand*, p. 6). The following discussion excludes data for Alaska.

44

The evidence on the diversion of gas to the intrastate market has been collected by the FPC[3] and analyzed for the Permian Basin area by Celia Star Gody of Foster Associates, Inc.[4] Table 3 summarizes data she prepared for her testimony before the FPC. On the basis of these data, she stated:

The extent of the reversal from interstate to intrastate sales is striking. . . . The intrastate market continued to take nearly all available supplies in 1969 and the first half of 1970. . . . Thus, the conspicuous feature of market behavior has been the diversion of nearly all new supplies to the intrastate portion of the market.[5]

This effect was apparently quite pervasive, judging from pipeline companies' complaints to the FPC about their inability to bid reserves away from the intrastate market.[6]

Table 3
DISTRIBUTION OF NEW CONTRACT COMMITMENTS BETWEEN INTERSTATE AND INTRASTATE SALES, LARGE PRODUCERS, PERMIAN BASIN AREA, 1966-70

Year	Percentage Committed Interstate	Percentage Committed Intrastate
1966	83.7	16.3
1967	78.2	21.8
1968	12.8	87.2
1969	16.7	83.3
1970 (6 months)	9.1	90.9

Source: Celia Star Gody, *Prepared Testimony*, FPC Docket No. AR70-1 et al. (Washington, D. C.: Foster Associates, Inc., June 1971), Exhibit No. (CSG-1), Chart 3, p. 6.

---

[3] FPC, *Nationwide Investigation*, Docket No. R-389A, September 9, 1970 and November 8, 1971. The 1970 study reported information on intrastate sales by seventy large, regulated gas producers whose individual sales were in excess of 10 Bcf annually; the 1971 study included sixty-nine such companies.

[4] Celia Star Gody, *Prepared Testimony*, FPC Docket No. AR70-1 (Washington: Foster Associates, Inc., June 1971).

[5] Ibid., pp. 9-10.

[6] The diversion of gas from the interstate pipelines makes the frequently heard argument that the "gas shortage" is a result of industry-produced reserve statistics a moot point. Even if independent producers withheld information to the AGA committees or revised their previous estimates of "recoverable reserves" downward, the effect would be the same: in the absence of economic incentives these producers are not committing gas to the interstate market. Higher interstate gas prices should increase the amount of gas committed to the interstate market as producers commit previously undeclared reserves (if any) and as new reserves are discovered.

A rough idea of the extent and timing of this diversion for the entire United States can be obtained by comparing the yearly gross additions to pipeline reserves as reported to the FPC with the yearly gross additions to total U.S. reserves as reported by the AGA. (The AGA data are adjusted to exclude those states where no inter-state pipeline reserves were reported.) As Table 4 shows, with the exception of 1967, the interstate pipelines were able to obtain an increased proportion of new gas discoveries each year from 1964 to 1968. Thereafter, and most strikingly after 1969, there was a large reduction in the amount of new gas committed to the inter-state market. While the diversion of gas from the interstate pipe-lines has been great, it apparently did not occur as early in other areas as it did in the Permian Basin—probably because this area's rates were the first to be settled through the area rate hearing process and were set at more restrictive limits than the rates for other areas. Permian Basin ceiling rates remained constant at 16.09¢/Mcf from 1961 to August 1965 and were then set at 15.58¢

Table 4

GROSS ADDITIONS COMMITTED TO INTERSTATE NATURAL GAS PIPELINES, 1964-71

| Year | Trillions of Cubic Feet of Gas | | Percent of Gross Additions Committed to Interstate Market[b] |
	Interstate pipeline gross additions	Adjusted AGA gross additions[a]	
1964	10.6	19.4	55.0
1965	13.3	20.9	63.6
1966	14.2	18.8	75.4
1967	14.8	21.3	69.3
1968	9.5	12.1	78.0
1969	6.1	8.4	72.6
1970	0.04	11.9	0.3
1971	2.0	9.3	21.3
1972	− 0.24	9.0	0

[a] Adjusted data exclude Alaska, California, Illinois, Indiana, and Michigan where no gas was reported on Forms 15 and 15-A.

[b] Percentage committed = 100 x (pipeline gross additions ÷ AGA gross additions).

Source: Interstate pipeline gross additions and adjusted AGA gross additions: FPC, *Gas Supplies of Pipeline Companies,* Table 4, p. 10.

through 1969.[7] The Foster Associates' new contract prices for the Permian Basin were below the ceiling rates from 1962 through 1964 but were above the ceiling rates for all years after 1964.

The AGA reserve data used here, which include interstate and intrastate gas, show a similar declining trend in reserves, both absolutely and relative to production. The decline in reserves evidenced by the AGA data has been summarized by a recent FPC study:

> During the past ten years, cumulative reserve additions have been slightly less than cumulative production, replacing 97 percent of the gas produced, while during the last three years (1968-1970) reserve additions have replaced only about 51 percent of the gas that has been produced.[8]

Additional evidence that the FPC's policies have resulted in a real shortage may be found in the curtailments of gas service by interstate pipelines. Recent figures for curtailments under "firm" delivery contracts show that the amount of gas curtailed by major interstate pipelines has increased from 343.5 Bcf in 1971[9] to 555.4 Bcf in 1972 (April through October only)[10] and 966.3 Bcf in 1973 (April through October only).[11] For the 1973-74 heating season (November through March), the pipeline companies estimate they will have to curtail about 753 Bcf, an increase of 33.3 percent from the actual 1972-73 winter curtailments of 564.7 Bcf.[12] For the yearly period September 1973 through August 1974, the pipelines now estimate they will have to curtail 53.1 percent more than the 1,031 Bcf they actually curtailed during the previous year.[13] These estimates understate the reductions in deliveries of gas since they do not include curtailments of "interruptible" sales contracts. Interruptible curtailments during the year from September 1972 through August 1973 were 284.9 Bcf. It is estimated they will be 17.2 percent greater (334.0 Bcf) for the year from September 1973 through August 1974.[14]

---

[7] Khazzoom, *Econometric Model of U.S. Natural Gas Supply,* Table A-4.

[8] FPC, *National Gas Supply and Demand,* p. 7.

[9] *FPC News,* vol. 5, no. 48 (December 1, 1972), p. 1.

[10] FPC News Release No. 19640, September 17, 1973, Schedule I.

[11] Ibid., Schedule II. This figure includes estimated curtailments for August through October.

[12] FPC News Release No. 20019, January 31, 1974, Schedule II; 753 Bcf is approximately 3.3 percent of 1972 total marketed production of natural gas.

[13] Ibid., Schedule I.

[14] Ibid., Schedule IV, p. 2.

When effective price controls create excess demand, there will be an increased demand for substitutes. The increased attention being given to higher-priced substitutes for natural gas is ample evidence that a substantial shortage now exists. Of the substitutes for domestically produced pipeline-quality gas, liquified natural gas (LNG) imported by ship from the Middle East is now the most important. There are several applications now before the FPC for importation of LNG along the Atlantic seaboard.[15] The number of LNG ships in service has increased from five in 1968 to nine in 1972. As of August 1, 1972, there were twenty-six LNG ships on order.[16] Current imports of Algerian LNG cost the Boston Gas Co. $1.14/Mcf, and imports by truck from Canada to the Boston-New York area range in price from $1.12 to $2.20. Under the approved El Paso import application,[17] gas would be sold at about $1/Mcf on the East Coast, about twice the present cost of pipeline gas in the same area.[18]

Synthetic natural gas (SNG) from coal is considered another likely possibility, although the technology for converting coal to pipeline-quality gas has not been perfected. One estimate set the cost range of SNG between 75¢ and $1.10/Mcf,[19] but a later project application by El Paso Natural Gas Company estimated the cost at $1.21/Mcf.[20]

Natural gas from new discoveries in Alaska has also been considered as a supplement to gas produced in the contiguous states. The FPC has estimated the cost of Alaskan gas at $1.18 to $1.35/Mcf, although there is great uncertainty as to what the field price of Alaskan gas will be.[21] Estimates of transportation costs from Alaska have been made by the Gas Arctic Systems Study Group: 31¢/Mcf to Idaho and 43¢/Mcf to Minnesota by way of a 1,550-mile 48-inch pipeline across the Yukon and Northwest Territories.[22] The Moun-

[15] FPC, *Annual Report, 1972*, Appendix E.

[16] "The LNG Carrier: A Product of the Growing Energy Crisis," *Marine Engineering/Log*, vol. 77, no. 10 (September 1972), Table 1, p. 39.

[17] FPC, Columbia LNG Corp. et al., Docket Nos. CP71-68 et al., Opinion No. 622, issued June 28, 1972.

[18] By the use of 1969 cost and quantity figures for six pipeline companies which serve areas from North Carolina through New Hampshire and buy all their gas from larger pipeline companies, a weighted average "city gate" price of 43.6¢/Mcf was computed. FPC, *Statistics of Interstate Natural Gas Pipeline Companies, 1969* (Washington, D.C.: Government Printing Office, 1970).

[19] FPC, *National Gas Supply and Demand*, pp. 84-90.

[20] *FPC News*, vol. 5, no. 48 (December 1, 1972), p. 8.

[21] FPC, Columbia LNG Corp. et al., Docket Nos. CP71-68.

[22] FPC, *National Gas Supply and Demand*, pp. 102-104.

tain Pacific Project, a similar pipeline system through Canada, had estimated transportation costs of 40¢ to Seattle, 48¢ to San Francisco, and 54¢ to Los Angeles.[23] In 1972, the average cost of all natural gas consumed in the state of Washington was 78¢ and in California 66¢.[24] A more recent FPC estimate places the transportation costs of Canadian Arctic gas at 80¢ to $1.00/Mcf.[25]

A comparison of the estimated cost per BTU in 1971 for substitute sources of energy is presented in Table 5. The table shows

Table 5
COSTS OF ALTERNATIVE SOURCES OF ENERGY, ACTUAL AND ESTIMATED

Sources of Energy	Cost per Million BTUs
Methanol from coal	$1.73
SNG from coal	$1.26-$1.56 [a]
Imported LNG [b]	$1.34
Syncrude from oil shale	$1.17
Canadian Arctic gas, by pipeline	$1.12-$1.32
Natural gas—average city gate [c]	$ .51
Natural gas—average wellhead [d]	$ .23
Natural gas—new at wellhead [e]	$ .41
For electrical generation (February 1974)	
Fuel oil	$1.87
Coal	$ .57
Natural gas	$ .40

[a] El Paso Natural Gas estimates the cost from its recently approved New Mexico gas-from-coal complex will be $1.51 for the first year and $1.25/Mcf over the life of the plant (*Wall Street Journal*, June 24, 1974).

[b] Based on average LNG import cost of $1.38/Mcf and a conversion factor of 1027 BTU/cubic foot of gas.

[c] Based on 51.87¢/Mcf average sales by major interstate pipeline companies during the twelve months ending March 1974.

[d] Based on 23.53¢/Mcf average cost of purchases from domestic producers by major interstate pipeline companies during the twelve months ending March 1974.

[e] Based on the FPC's new 42¢/Mcf price ceiling and a conversion factor of 1027 BTU/cubic foot of gas.

Source: *Technology Review*, edited at Massachusetts Institute of Technology, May 1974, p. 45; FPC News Releases No. 20372 and 20378, June 6, 1974.

[23] Ibid., p. 105.

[24] Bureau of Mines, "Natural Gas Production and Consumption: 1972," *Mineral Industry Surveys* (Washington, D.C.: Division of Fossil Fuels, September 7, 1973), Table 6.

[25] FPC, "Future Gas Supplies from Alternate Sources," *National Gas Survey*, June 1974, Chapter 10, p. 55.

the higher cost of most alternative energy sources. Coal is the most likely alternative source of cheap energy. It exists in abundant supply but the externalities connected with its burning and extraction make it a less desired source of energy than natural gas at the same price.[26]

For comparison, the model used here suggests that in the absence of regulation in the 1960s additional supplies of natural gas could have been obtained in the southwestern producing states at constant prices near 30¢/Mcf. This estimate is based on the conditions existing in the industry before 1960, and it is likely that structural conditions have changed in recent years so that the current cost of additional gas reserves may be greater than 30¢/Mcf. Since domestic drilling for both oil and gas declined during the 1960s, the stock of known but undrilled prospects for gas is lower now than in the 1950s.[27] Moreover, additional supplies of domestic gas are likely to be found at greater depths than present supplies or offshore where drilling costs are approximately three times higher than they are on land ($71/foot offshore compared to $24/foot for land-based drilling).[28] Even if the estimated 30¢ price is doubled to allow for structural change, domestically produced natural gas is still approximately half the cost of available substitutes for pipeline-quality gas. These conditions have led FPC Commissioner Moody to declare that it is a "fundamental absurdity" for the FPC to authorize LNG imports at $1.00/Mcf while restricting pipeline payments to domestic producers to 26¢/Mcf.[29]

It is interesting to note that Edmund Kitch, in his 1968 article, predicted that area price control would eventually cause supply and rationing problems.

In 1960 the Commission clamped a ceiling on the field market only after the upward price trend of the fifties resulting from increased transmission efficiencies and competition had halted. But the next time an upward shift in the field market occurs the Commission will be firmly astride the field market. It will respond just as slowly as

---

[26] Severe restrictions and sometimes outright prohibition of the use of coal by many cities have increased the demand for natural gas relative to coal.

[27] Erickson and Spann, "Supply Response in a Regulated Industry."

[28] IPAA, *Joint Association Survey of the U.S. Oil and Gas Producing Industry, 1972.*

[29] *FPC News,* vol. 5, no. 27 (July 7, 1972), p. 7. See also Council of Economic Advisers, *Economic Report of the President, 1971* (Washington, D.C.: Government Printing Office, 1972), p. 122, and the discussion below (pp. 54-56) where this model is used to compare the cost of domestic gas to the cost of imported substitutes.

it has in the past. The tragedy is that the next increase may be another increase in the field price, like the increase of the 1950's, without any corresponding increase in the delivered cost of gas to consumers. . . .

In the field market the regulation will only cause the loss of gas which would otherwise be produced. In the consumer markets the possible consequences are even more disturbing. The transportation system is subject to rate base regulation which prevents price increases due to scarcity. Therefore, when and if the price ceiling in the field becomes economically effective, the price ceiling will be transmitted forward to the consuming market. There will be a shortage.[30]

In other words, Kitch predicted in 1968 that the response to the next gas crisis would be similar to the rationing that accompanied price controls during World War II rather than being a switch to alternative energy sources like that which occurred in the earlier Appalachian crisis. He concluded that "the gas supply system simply does not lend itself to enforceable rationing. Price control without rationing creates a market crisis which, in the case of natural gas, can literally be disastrous." [31]

The Policy for Stimulating Domestic Exploration

The effects of area regulation have not been completely ignored by the FPC, although, as Kitch predicted, the commission's response has been slow. Beginning in 1969 the commission used its own evidence of the gas shortage to modify area rate regulation and to stimulate exploration for and development of new reserves. This change in attitude is reflected in the recent opinion on area rates in the Appalachian-Illinois Basin areas: "In retrospect, we find that the rates established in 1970 did not produce the necessary results, and the public interest clearly requires that we avoid that which experience has shown to be futile." [32]

The model given here can be used to evaluate one aspect of the FPC's attempt to stimulate additional reserves. Using the pre-regulation estimated coefficients, we can estimate the response in the stock of reserves to increases in new-contract gas prices. We must make realistic assumptions to determine the price of new gas

---

[30] Kitch, "Regulation of Field Market," pp. 278-279.

[31] Ibid., p. 279.

[32] FPC, Area Rate for the Appalachian and Illinois Basin Areas, Docket No. R-371, Opinion No. 639, issued December 12, 1972, p. 12.

and insert the price we come up with into the estimating equation for the stock of reserves (R_t). The results for this procedure are given in Table 6.[33] The second column shows that if the FPC holds the line at the approximate 1972 ceiling rates of 26¢,[34] the stock of reserves will increase about 7 percent by 1980, with most of this increase occurring by 1975. If market rates increase to 50¢ in 1973 and remain at this level (column 3), reserves should increase by 38 percent. In these two cases (columns 2 and 3) reserves would increase at a decreasing rate. Alternatively, reserves would increase at an increasing rate if the price of gas is assumed to increase by a fixed percentage yearly. When the price of gas is assumed to increase annually after 1972 at 5, 10, and 15 percent, the percentage response in the stock of reserves by 1980 is 25, 49, and 81 percent respectively.

While it is not known exactly how the structural parameters have changed from the period before 1960 to the period after 1972, the important point here is that the industry can be expected to respond to price increases. Indeed, there is some indication that a turnaround in exploration activity for gas may have already occurred. Data on well-drilling activity for 1973 indicate that completed gas wells were up 65 percent from 1971 whereas oil well completions were down 17 percent in the same two year period.[35] Some sources argue that this response is more the result of increased intrastate rates than of the FPC's new policies.[36]

A retarding effect on exploration is also likely because of continuing uncertainty about the future of FPC field price regulation. All but one of the recent area rate proceedings are now under attack in the courts, and some congressmen are complaining about the

---

[33] The estimating equation for (R_t) is

$$R_t = 34.92 + 2.03\ PG_t{}^* - 1.21\ PO_t + .28\ PL_t + .75\ R_{t-1}.$$

When available for the years 1970-73, actual exogenous data for PG, PO, and PL were used. After 1973, PO and PL were assumed to increase in real terms at 3 percent per year.

[34] FPC, *Annual Report, 1971*, p. 37-43.

[35] IPAA, *Petroleum Statistics, 1974*. These figures indicate considerable directionality in the search for petroleum.

[36] Note the following comment by Gilbert Burck in "The FPC Is Backing Away from the Wellhead," *Fortune*, vol. 86, no. 5 (November 1972), p. 180:
Many wildcatters turn up their noses at the new FPC policy because it makes no provision for the future renegotiation of prices, and these operators believe that prices will keep on moving up. What has principally spurred the wildcatters is the rising price of unregulated intrastate gas, which is now fetching as much as 52 cents a thousand cubic feet. Some wildcatters are dreaming of 75-cent gas; their zeal proves, once again, that higher prices can spur exploration and development.

Table 6

ESTIMATED RESPONSE OF GAS RESERVES TO NEW CONTRACT PRICES, 1970-80

Year	Reserves When Prices Equal:		Price Increases at 5% from 26¢ in 1972		Price Increases at 10% from 26¢ in 1972		Price Increases at 15% from 26¢ in 1972	
	26¢ᵃ	50¢ᵇ	Pricesᶜ	Reserves	Pricesᶜ	Reserves	Pricesᶜ	Reserves
1970	276.2	276.2	18.5	276.2	18.5	276.2	18.5	276.2
1971	279.4	279.4	19.7	279.4	19.7	279.4	19.7	279.4
1972	283.7	283.7	20.6	283.7	20.6	283.7	20.6	283.7
1973	287.1	311.2	21.6	289.2	22.6	291.2	23.7	293.3
1974	289.5	331.6	22.7	295.4	24.9	301.4	27.2	307.7
1975	291.3	346.9	23.8	302.2	27.4	314.0	31.3	326.6
1976	292.6	358.2	25.0	309.8	30.1	328.9	36.0	350.3
1977	293.5	366.7	26.3	317.9	33.1	346.2	41.4	378.9
1978	294.1	372.9	27.6	326.5	36.4	365.7	47.6	412.8
1979	294.4	377.5	28.9	335.7	40.1	387.7	54.7	452.6
1980	294.7	380.9	30.7	345.5	44.1	412.2	62.9	499.0

ᵃ 26¢ is equal to 20.6¢ in 1957-59 dollars. The 1973 wholesale price index is 154.16.

ᵇ 50¢ is equal to 32¢ in 1957-59 dollars.

ᶜ All new contract price (PG*) projections are in constant dollars (1957-59 = 100). For the period 1969-72, prices are assumed to increase from 19.7¢ to 26¢ (20.6¢ deflated), figures which approximate the actual increase.

Source: See Appendix A.

FPC's changes in policy.[37] The commission discussed this uncertainty in its order establishing "optional pricing."

> Because our area rate orders remain under attack, at the present time a producer, even if he is willing to sell at the rates fixed in such opinions, does not know that those rates will be affirmed on appeal. . . . there is no assurance at the present time that a producer may not ultimately have to refund some of an initial rate based on a just and reasonable determination and upon which the producer relied when it dedicated a new gas supply to the interstate market. In short, after some 18 years of producer regulation, the producer does not know how much it can lawfully charge for sales on natural gas in interstate commerce nor how much it will get if it develops and sells new gas to the interstate market. The producer knows for sure only that once it sells in interstate commerce it cannot stop deliveries.[38]

In an attempt to reduce some of this uncertainty, the FPC is officially supporting "sanctity of contract" legislation whereby the commission would be prevented from changing any of the provisions of a contract it had previously approved.

The Cost of Domestic and Imported Gas Supplies

The model can be used to make estimates of the costs of obtaining gas domestically in an unregulated market and of importing substitutes such as LNG.[39] The basic procedure (used here for the years 1972-80) is to compute a price (P_1) and a quantity (Q_1) series under the assumption of no domestic price controls and no imports, and another price (P_2) and quantity (Q_2) series under the assumption of regulated domestic prices and imports costing \$1.00/Mcf.[40] The cost (C) of regulating domestic prices is then computed as follows:

---

[37] Ibid., p. 185. But this uncertainty has been reduced somewhat by two recent Supreme Court decisions upholding the FPC's higher area rates in southern Louisiana and the Texas Gulf Coast areas. *Wall Street Journal,* June 18, 1974, p. 4.

[38] FPC, *Optional Procedure for Certificating New Producer Sales of Natural Gas,* p. 9.

[39] For a discussion of the basic procedure, see P. W. MacAvoy, "The Effectiveness of the Federal Power Commission," *The Bell Journal of Economics and Management Science,* pp. 274-275.

[40] A \$1.00/Mcf cost of imported LNG is not unreasonable given current costs and recent estimates. See the article by R. Bruce Foster in Brown, *Regulation of Natural Gas Producing Industry,* pp. 63-89. The average cost of 1972 LNG imports was \$1.38 (*FPC News,* June 15, 1973, Table 6, p. 5).

$$C = (P_2 - P_1) Q_2 + \frac{1}{2}(P_2 - P_1) (Q_1 - Q_2).$$

The equation measures two elements of cost imposed on the consumer by regulation. If expensive, imported LNG is used instead of the cheaper, new domestic gas which would become available in an unregulated market, the consumer will pay a higher price for gas (P_2 rather than P_1) and use a smaller quantity (Q_2). The first term in the equation measures the excess cost of the smaller quantity used resulting from the higher price paid for imported LNG. In addition, consumers lose the benefits of the larger quantity of gas (Q_1) they would consume at the lower price for new gas (P_1) that would prevail in the absence of regulation. This additional loss from regulation is measured by the second term in the equation. The assumptions and procedure used to estimate these prices and quantities are explained in Appendix B. The results are presented in Table 7.

Table 7

ESTIMATED COST OF
IMPORTED VERSUS DOMESTIC GAS, 1972-80

Year	Unregulated Domestic Field Market		Regulated Domestic Market with Imported LNG		Cost of Regulation and Imports [c]
	Price (P_1) [a]	Quantity (Q_1) [b]	Price (P_2) [a]	Quantity (Q_2) [b]	(millions of 1973 dollars)
1972	27.5	26.1	28.0	26.1	$139.3
1973	28.4	27.4	29.8	27.2	376.1
1974	29.8	28.4	32.6	27.6	784.8
1975	30.3	28.3	33.1	26.3	760.2
1976	31.5	28.8	33.7	26.8	640.4
1977	31.7	28.2	34.2	26.9	691.8
1978	32.7	28.7	34.7	27.2	565.4
1979	32.9	28.1	35.2	27.4	643.2
1980	33.7	28.7	35.5	27.5	512.2

[a] (P_1) and (P_2): Average price of domestic field consumption, ¢/Mcf. The average price (P_t) is the ten-year average of new contract prices (PG_{t-9}) to (PG_t) where actual new contract prices are used from 1963-71 and PG^* is used from 1972 through 1980.

[b] (Q_1) and (Q_2): Trillions of cubic feet. The initial volume of 26.113 Tcf in 1972 is from the FRC projection. R_{71} used in the computations is 247.44 Tcf, the actual level of reserves for the contiguous forty-eight states.

[c] Figures may not add due to rounding.

The model shows that the cost (loss in consumer surplus) of importing LNG to make up for the domestic shortage created by regulation would average $657 million each year over the seven years, 1974-80. If the structure of the industry has actually changed since the 1950s so that additional domestic gas can only be found at prices higher than the approximately 30¢ established by the model, then these projections underestimate the true cost of obtaining additional domestic gas. In any case it can be concluded that the United States will have to pay a great deal more for energy in the next decade than it has paid in the past. Ironically, the additional cost will be less if the FPC and the Congress allow the field price of gas to rise.

Distribution of the Benefits of Field Market Regulation

To the extent that area rate regulation restricted the price for field gas, a benefit was created for the purchasers of the gas that was sold at the lower prices. It was the avowed purpose of FPC regulation that this gain be passed on to residential consumers of natural gas. Some evidence on how this gain was actually distributed can be obtained by examining rates of return and stock prices for different classes of regulated natural gas companies and other regulated utilities. These comparisons may be made because of similarities in the form of regulation to which these utilities are subject, as well as some similarities in costs and demand conditions.

Figures 7 through 10 and Tables 8 through 11 present rates of return for several classifications of natural gas companies and other utilities. The most notable feature of these data is the divergence of rates of return for gas companies from rates of return for electric and telephone utilities since 1965. The fact that the regulated pipeline companies' rates of return increased in the late 1960s while rates of return for other utilities declined is consistent with the view that field market regulation was not effective until after 1967. Since gas purchase costs average about 80 percent of a pipeline's total operation and maintenance expenses, and since the proportion of gas coming from pre-1967 contracts is continually declining, the effect of binding area rates has been a continuous increase in the net saving in gas purchase costs for regulated interstate pipelines since 1967. The excess demand for gas was not completely reflected in retail market prices because pipeline and distribution companies were subject to one form or another of rate-base regulation. But,

Figure 7

CASH FLOW AS A PERCENT OF NET UTILITY PLANT

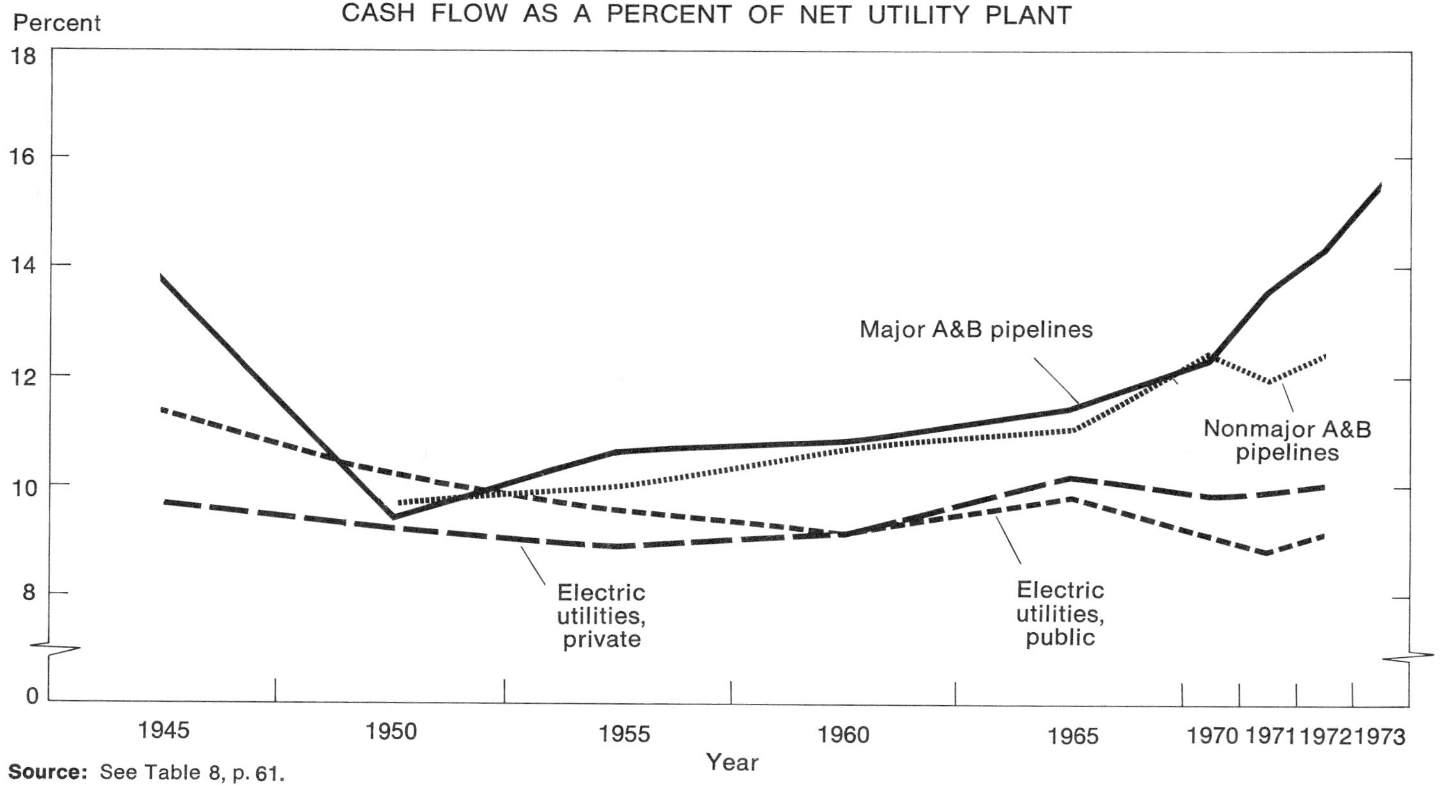

Source: See Table 8, p. 61.

57

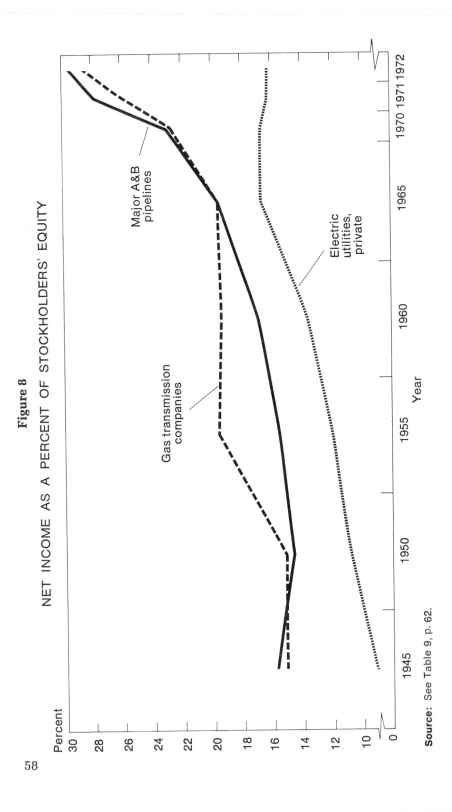

Figure 8

NET INCOME AS A PERCENT OF STOCKHOLDERS' EQUITY

Percent

Major A&B
pipelines

Gas transmission
companies

Electric
utilities,
private

Year

Source: See Table 9, p. 62.

58

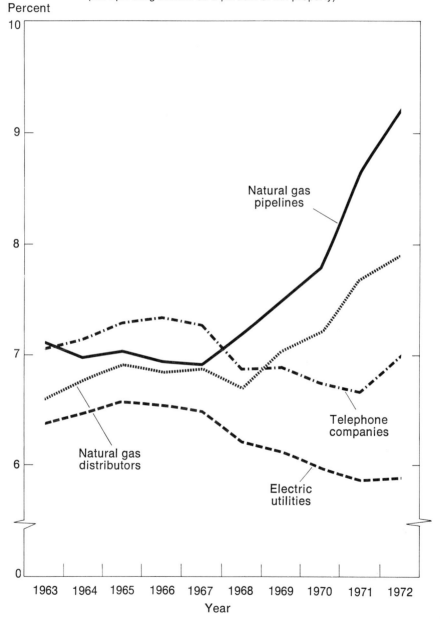

Figure 9

STANDARD AND POOR'S PERCENT EARNED
ON NET PROPERTY
(net operating income as a percent of net property)

Percent

Natural gas
pipelines

Telephone
companies

Natural gas
distributors

Electric
utilities

Year

Source: See Table 10, p. 62.

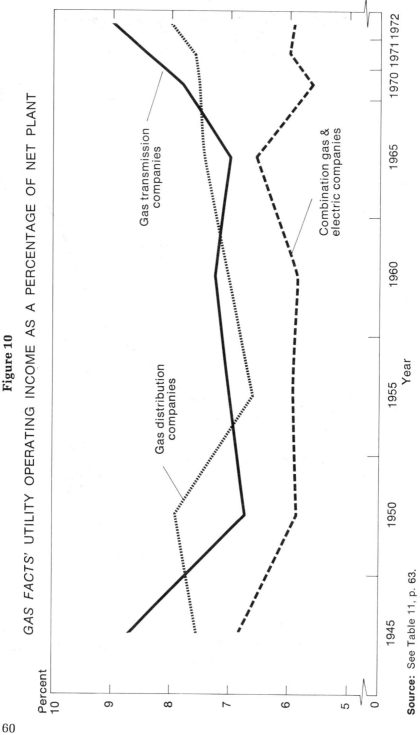

Figure 10

GAS FACTS' UTILITY OPERATING INCOME AS A PERCENTAGE OF NET PLANT

Gas transmission companies

Combination gas & electric companies

Gas distribution companies

Percent

Year

Source: See Table 11, p. 63.

60

Table 8

UTILITY RATES OF RETURN: CASH FLOW[a] AS A PERCENT OF NET UTILITY PLANT, 1945-73

Year	Major A&B Gas Pipelines	Gas Transmission Companies	Non-Major Gas Pipelines	Electric Utilities, Private	Electric Utilities, Public
1945	13.7	13.6	—	9.7	11.4[b]
1950	9.4	9.7	9.7	9.2	10.2
1955	10.6	10.6	10.0	8.9	9.6
1960	10.8	11.2	10.7	9.1	9.1
1965	11.4	11.2	11.1	10.2	9.8
1970	12.3	12.2	12.4	9.8	9.1
1971	13.5	13.3	12.0	9.9	8.8
1972	14.3	14.3	12.4	10.0	9.1
1973	15.5	n.a.	n.a.	n.a.	n.a.

[a] Cash flow for the electric utilities is net income plus depreciation, amortization, depletion, and total interest payments. To avoid the possibility that the divergent rates of return were due to more diversification among gas pipelines than among other types of utilities, other income and extraordinary items have been subtracted from the net income of gas pipeline companies. This means that the rates of return for electric utilities are overstated relative to those for gas pipelines.

[b] 1946 data.

Source: Major and nonmajor gas pipelines: FPC, *Statistics of Interstate Natural Gas Pipeline Companies, 1945, 1972,* and *FPC News,* vol. 7, no. 10 (March 8, 1974), p. 3. Gas transmission companies: AGA, *Gas Facts, 1971-1972 Data,* Tables 103 and 115. Electric utilities, private: FPC, *Statistics of Privately Owned Electric Utilities in the United States, 1971,* Tables 10 and 13, and *FPC News,* vol. 7, no. 21 (May 24, 1974), p. 26. Electric utilities, public: FPC, *Statistics of Publicly Owned Electric Utilities in the United States, 1972,* Tables 11 and 14.

as Professor MacAvoy has shown, for the period 1962-68,[41] the pipelines were able to increase the proportion of sales to unregulated industrial customers, thus increasing their revenue and rates of return.[42] As Professor MacAvoy puts it:

The pipelines in a period of short supply additions seem to have been allocating relatively more of this new gas to

[41] Paul W. MacAvoy, "The Regulation Induced Shortage of Natural Gas," *Journal of Law and Economics,* vol. 14, no. 1 (April 1971), pp. 190-197. This result has also been found by the FPC's "Wein study," as discussed in Steele, *Use of Econometric Models,* pp. 48-49.

[42] This reallocation may have been an ongoing process resulting from the exemption of industrial sales from regulation. It would be interesting to see if the rate of reallocation to industrial users increased after 1967 as this analysis indicates.

Table 9

UTILITY RATES OF RETURN: NET INCOME AS A PERCENT OF STOCKHOLDERS' EQUITY, 1945-72 [a]

Year	Major A&B Gas Pipelines	Gas Transmission Companies	Electric Utilities, Private
1945	15.8	15.2	9.0
1950	14.5	15.2	10.8
1955	15.5	19.6	12.0
1960	16.7	19.3	13.5
1965	19.5	19.5	16.5
1970	22.9	22.6	16.4
1971	27.5	25.8	16.1
1972	29.3	28.4	16.1

[a] Stockholders' equity is defined as common stock plus preferred stock issued.

Source: Gas pipelines: FPC, *Statistics of Interstate Natural Gas Pipeline Companies,* various years. Transmission companies: AGA, *Gas Facts, 1972 Data,* Tables 103 and 115. Electric utilities: FPC, *Statistics of Privately Owned Electric Utilities in the United States, 1970,* Tables 10 and 13, and *FPC News,* vol. 7, no. 21 (May 24, 1974), pp. 26-27.

Table 10

UTILITY RATES OF RETURN: STANDARD AND POOR'S PERCENT EARNED ON NET PROPERTY, 1963-72 [a]

Year	Natural Gas Pipelines	Natural Gas Distributors	Electric Utilities	Telephone Companies
1963	7.11	6.60	6.38	7.05
1964	6.98	6.76	6.46	7.13
1965	7.02	6.90	6.56	7.29
1966	6.95	6.83	6.53	7.32
1967	6.91	6.87	6.49	7.26
1968	7.18	6.69	6.21	6.86
1969	7.47	7.02	6.12	6.89
1970	7.78	7.20	5.97	6.74
1971	8.64	7.66	5.86	6.66
1972	9.20	7.89	5.88	6.96

[a] Net operating income as percent of net property.

Source: Standard and Poor's *Industry Surveys,* Composite Industry Data, 1973.

Table 11

UTILITY RATES OF RETURN: *GAS FACTS'* UTILITY OPERATING
INCOME AS A PERCENT OF NET PLANT, 1945-72

Year	Natural Gas Transmission Companies	Natural Gas Distribution Companies	Combination Natural Gas & Electric Distribution Companies
1945	8.7	7.5	6.8
1950	6.7	7.9	5.8
1955	7.0	6.6	5.9
1960	7.3	7.0	5.8
1965	7.0	7.4	6.5
1970	7.8	7.5	5.6
1971	8.4	7.6	6.0
1972	9.0	8.0	5.9

Source: AGA, *Gas Facts, 1972 Data,* Tables 123, 124, and 126.

industrial users, probably as a result of loose or non-existent regulation of industrial resale, while there was strong regulation on home resale. The regulated rates for deliveries to retail public utility companies increased only when field gas prices or delivery costs changed, and ceiling prices in the field greatly limited these increases.[43]

The evidence on rates of return also supports the conclusion that among gas utilities those regulated by the FPC have received relatively more of the benefits of lower field prices than those not regulated by the FPC. Figures 9 and 10 give time series of operating income as a percent of net plant.[44] The series in Figure 10 show that the rates of return of gas transmission companies[45] have increased relative to the rates of return for gas distribution companies and combination gas and electric distribution companies. The

---

[43] MacAvoy, "Regulation Induced Shortage of Natural Gas," pp. 196-197.

[44] The rates differ because Standard and Poor's and the AGA use different sets of firms to define the broad categories.

[45] Gas transmission companies are defined by the AGA as those companies for which 95 percent of total revenues are from gas sales for resale and for which 95 percent of their gas mains are engaged in transmission. While this category may include some non-FPC-regulated intrastate pipelines, it is a more restrictive definition than the FPC's major class A and B pipelines (those whose sales for resale exceed 50 Bcf per year).

difference between the rates of return for pipeline companies and distribution companies is apparent in Figure 9. Pipeline returns increased more rapidly after 1967 than distribution company returns.[46] Figures 8 and 9 also show clearly the widening post-1967 gap between natural gas and other regulated utility rates of return.

Professor MacAvoy has also argued that FPC regulation benefited large established pipelines at the expense of small less-established pipelines.[47] Figure 7, which compares rates of return of large pipelines and small pipelines, supports this argument (the overlapping category of gas transmission companies is not shown). The returns of the larger regulated companies, after having paralleled those of the smaller companies for twenty-five years, increased substantially more than the returns to the smaller companies after 1970. This divergence is not the result of earnings from nonutility activities, because the rates of return for all three categories of pipelines were computed in such a way as to exclude other income and extraordinary items from cash flow. (In the denominator net gas utility plant was used instead of total utility plant.)

If regulated pipeline companies benefited from field market price controls, we would expect to see the equity prices of these companies increasing more than those of natural gas distribution companies and other regulated utilities. Table 12 gives index numbers computed from Moody's and Standard and Poor's data on average stock prices for composite groups of utilities. Even though the two investment services use different samples the relative gain in the value of pipeline company stocks is evident in both cases. As the second and fourth columns clearly show, the price of pipeline company stocks as a group increased while the prices of all other classifications of utility stocks, including those for gas distribution companies (columns 3 and 5), declined. If we include all dividends and look at the outcome of an investment in each of these groups of utilities, we can see from Table 13 that the dollar value of an investment in pipeline companies would have increased

---

[46] It is interesting to note that pipeline rates of return began to increase in 1968, exactly the year that this model suggests area rate regulation would have begun to restrict the field prices paid by regulated interstate pipelines.

[47] Paul W. MacAvoy, "The Formal Work-Product of the Federal Power Commission," *The Bell Journal of Economics and Management Science*, vol. 2, no. 1 (Spring 1971), pp. 390–391. MacAvoy's contention is that area rates would lower the gas purchase costs of the older more-established pipelines that did not have exploration and development programs and that were in a position to purchase the limited supplies. This would particularly limit the growth of those newer pipelines still actively engaged in developing resale markets.

Table 12

INDEX OF UTILITY STOCK PRICES, MAJOR
REGULATED UTILITY GROUPS, 1965-74
(1965 = 100)

	Moody's		Standard and Poor's			
Year	Gas transmission companies	Gas distribution companies	Gas pipelines	Gas distributors	Electric utilities	Telephone companies
1965	100	100	100	100	100	100
1966	89.3	88.0	93.4	86.9	87.5	88.1
1967	96.9	77.7	101.8	82.1	85.5	87.9
1968	108.8	76.9	116.2	86.7	87.4	82.5
1969	102.2	72.7	113.0	81.3	79.8	81.2
1970	94.4	68.6	110.8	81.0	68.7	71.1
1971	105.5	72.7	120.3	87.2	75.1	72.5
1972	107.1	69.0	131.0	87.1	71.0	73.6
1973	104.7	71.1	122.5	82.4	63.1	75.3
1974	111.4 a	70.3 a	—	—	—	—
Number of companies	39-47	84-109	7	11	35	6

a March 2, 1974.

Source: Index numbers computed from composite $/share figures as follows: Moody's *Public Utility Manual, 1973,* pp. a14-15, and Moody's "News Reports," March 5, 1974, p. 1645; Standard and Poor's *Industry Surveys,* Composite Industry Data, 1973, and Standard and Poor's "Outlook," March 11, 1974, p. 888.

relative to both all other groups of utilities and to Standard and Poor's 60 utilities.[48] It appears that investors recognized the gain that was bestowed on regulated pipelines by the FPC.

While this evidence does not rule out the possibility that some benefit was passed on to gas consumers, it casts serious doubt on the contention that gas consumers have been the principal beneficiaries of field price regulation. In fact, the evidence is more consistent

[48] This procedure, which relies on market-determined stock prices and reinvests all dividends at current market prices, avoids having to rely on accounting rates of return. Since stock prices reflect all known information about each stock, the value of an investment in stocks will only change to reflect real economic changes. Any bias in accounting rates of return due to changing accounting rules or differential accounting practices among utilities would not be reflected in stock prices. See statement of Edward J. Mitchell before the Special Subcommittee on Integrated Oil Operations, Committee on Interior and Insular Affairs, United States Senate, February 21, 1974.

Table 13

OUTCOME OF $100 INVESTMENT IN FIVE COMPOSITE
UTILITY GROUPS, 1965-72 [a]

Year	Natural Gas Pipelines	Natural Gas Distributors	Electric Utilities	Telephone Companies	S&P's 60 Utilities
1965	$100	$100	$100	$100	$100
1966	97	89	92	92	93
1967	111	92	92	93	96
1968	136	103	97	94	101
1969	128	97	92	94	95
1970	143	110	89	90	94
1971	153	120	99	94	104
1972	166	122	91	109	114
Average annual return on investment	9.4%	3.1%	−1.3%	1.3%	2%

[a] The change in dollar value of a $100 investment made in 1965 assumes that all dividends are reinvested at current market prices. The dollar values of investments in each utility category were computed from Standard and Poor's stock data by Edward J. Mitchell. The above figures are based on the average of high, low, and closing stock prices.

Source: Standard and Poor's Compustat tapes.

with an hypothesis of "producer protection," whereby regulation benefits the regulated firms, than a "consumer protection" hypothesis, where the benefits of regulation accrue to consumers.[49] FPC field price regulation seems to have benefited regulated firms by keeping input prices down rather than by the more usual "producer protection" approach of keeping output prices up.

---

[49] For development of these hypotheses, see George J. Stigler, "The Theory of Economic Regulation," *The Bell Journal of Economics and Management Science,* vol. 2, no. 1 (Spring 1971), pp. 3-21; George J. Stigler, *Can Regulatory Agencies Protect the Consumer?* (Washington, D.C.: American Enterprise Institute, 1971); and William A. Jordan, "Producer Protection, Prior Market Structure and the Effects of Government Regulation," *Journal of Law and Economics,* vol. 15, no. 1 (April 1972), pp. 151-176.

5
REFORMING FIELD MARKET REGULATION

Using the behavior of the unregulated field market (pre-1960) as the basis for a model, this study has found that FPC area-rate regulation has had the effect of preventing the industry from responding to the increased demand that occurred in the late 1960s. Before 1967, abundant supplies of gas and declining pipeline demand caused field market prices to decline, thereby creating the illusion that area-rate regulation was a successful way to regulate a competitive industry. By the time the demand for gas began to increase after 1967, area-rate price controls were firmly in place. Their effect was to dissuade producers from searching for and developing new gas reserves. Prospective returns on investment in producing new gas reserves were too low to attract capital from alternative uses, given the price ceilings set by the FPC. As a result a large shortage of natural gas developed, eventually leading the FPC to allow some price increases in an attempt to alleviate the shortage. Despite this late attempt, the commission has been forced to ration the available supply.

This study has shown that, in the absence of field price regulation, natural gas producers would have responded to higher gas demand with increased search for and development of new reserves and the commitment of these reserves to the interstate market. Had field prices been allowed to rise, current consumption in both interstate and intrastate markets would have been smaller and natural gas reserves would have been more efficiently allocated over time. These findings lead us to the conclusion that the FPC has yet to devise a "successful" system of field market regulation for "providing adequate supplies at reasonable prices," as long as "reasonable prices" are interpreted to be prices which do not increase. The experience with field market controls shows clearly the inevitable long-run results of holding the price of a competitively produced product below the market equilibrium price. Some gain will accrue to existing consumers at the expense of retarded growth in service to new consumers, over consumption of expensive alternative fuels, and a reduction in the inventory of proven reserves.

Given these results, there seems to be no real case for continuing field market regulation. A proposal for the complete deregulation of the field market is discussed below. Even if there is no deregulation, several suggestions can be made for reforming field market regulation and are made here.

A Suggestion for Complete Deregulation

By complete deregulation I mean the removal of FPC authority over the provisions of all natural gas contracts negotiated between producers and pipelines. To do this would require a congressional amendment clarifying the ambiguous wording of the Natural Gas Act (see page 17 above). This action would eliminate price controls on both new and old contracts, thereby giving producers an incentive to develop old fields fully, to search for and develop new gas reserves, and to commit both old and new reserves to the interstate market.

Eliminating the FPC's regulatory control over natural gas contracts, both existing and future, would deregulate field prices and consequently reduce producers' uncertainty about future regulatory policy. This would give producers an added incentive to increase investment in natural gas exploration and development. However, if only new gas prices are deregulated, but not "old" gas prices, producers would be likely to interpret this as suggesting congressional intent to retain some control over natural gas prices. The result would be a smaller supply response to higher prices than would occur in the absence of such an interpretation.

The principal objection to the deregulation of field prices, and especially to the deregulation of prices for "old" gas, is that higher free market prices would bestow "unearned" or "windfall" profits on the owners of gas reserves. This is the standard "economic rent" argument which was persuasively presented by Professor Alfred Kahn in the Permian Basin hearings.[1] For the natural gas market, the economic rent argument can be presented in the following way. Once a quantity of gas is committed under long-term

---

[1] Permian Basin Area Rate Proceeding, AR 61-1, pp. 33-35, 50-51.

contract to the interstate market, that quantity and the prices to be charged for it are fixed—that is, the quantity of gas subject to that contract will in no way be affected by a change in the market price for gas (the supply curve is said to be perfectly inelastic). Under these conditions, it is argued an increase in the market demand for gas will increase the market value. If the contract allows for escalation, the owner of the gas will receive a "windfall profit" or economic rent. If the supply of old gas is not affected by price, it seems easy to conclude that, in Professor Kahn's words, "cost-based regulation, if intelligently applied, can diminish these windfalls, while interfering little or not at all with the flow of supply." [2]

However, given the evidence presented in this study regarding the decline in natural gas supply, something seems to be wrong with the economic rent argument when it is applied to the natural gas field market. The major difficulty with the argument can be found in Professor Kahn's own testimony: "The most familiar instances of economic rents are those accruing to the owners of completely nonreproducible goods like land. But in economic terms non-reproducibility is a matter of degree—of the degree of elasticity of supply." [3]

The reason Professor Kahn's argument leads to the unfortunate policy of different price ceilings on old and new gas is that it confuses the supply of gas under a fixed commitment with the more elastic market supply curve. To understand why price controls, even on old contracts, affect the supply of gas, it is necessary to look at the operation of a producing firm. Most producing firms are engaged in an ongoing program of exploration, development, and production. In any given year the exploration and development program will be adding reserves of gas to the firm's inventory of uncommitted gas. These reserves of gas can then be sold, typically under long-term contract, to the intrastate or interstate market. Annual revenues from the sale of gas must cover the firm's annual costs, including the cost of exploration and development of new gas, and provide a competitive rate of return on its investment. Price controls on the firm's old contracts will decrease its annual revenue but not its costs and thereby will reduce its rate of return and its ability and incentive to continue its exploration and development programs.

This is not to deny that some firms that own producing gas wells are not in any way engaged in exploration and development.

---

[2] Ibid.
[3] Ibid.

Firms in this category include those that have discontinued exploration and development as a result of past price controls. If the price of gas increases, these firms might earn an economic rent on their committed gas reserves. But the amount of gas owned by inactive firms (or inactive individuals) is small. In 1972, 98 percent of all reserves committed to the interstate market was owned by twenty-five major supply companies, and almost all of the amount committed (89.2 percent) was under independent producer contract.[4] Higher field prices resulting from complete deregulation could be expected to give the active producer companies added incentive to add to their inventory of gas reserves and might bring some of the now inactive producer companies back into business.

The economic rent argument as presented by Professor Kahn views the supply of gas as though it were a fixed quantity of gas in a reservoir. But the market supply curve, by standard economic definition, relates the quantities of gas that producers will place on the market during some time period to a set of prices. Given the nature of the gas-producing industry, there is no reason to believe that the market supply of natural gas will not be upward-sloping. Studies (including this one) have estimated the elasticity of domestically produced gas at approximately +.5—that is, for a 10 percent increase in field prices, reserves can be expected to increase 5 percent. On the basis of this past behavior of the industry, there seems to be no reason not to expect producers to respond to higher gas prices.[5]

Another argument against complete deregulation is a historical one. Opponents of the current attempts to deregulate the field market argue that it is "ironical" that large quantities of gas were dedicated to the interstate market during the 1960s under strict price controls while, during the 1970s, at a time when the FPC has been trying to raise the controlled field price and allow some exemptions to its regulations, interstate commitments have been declining.[6] This argument seems to imply that producers are not responsive to price—that they are more willing to sell gas in the interstate market when controlled prices are at a low level and less willing to sell gas when prices are allowed to increase.

---

[4] *FPC News,* October 5, 1973, p. 4.

[5] See also the discussion of economic rent by Hawkins, "Natural Gas Producing Industry," p. 162, where he concluded: "It is anything but clear that producers would earn rents in the absence of regulation."

[6] See the comments of former FPC Chairman Lee C. White in Phillips, "Energy Report/Congress Nears Showdown," p. 767.

This argument fails when one considers both the history of the field market and the effect of regulation on producers' expectations. The large quantities of gas committed in the early 1960s resulted from development of major discoveries of the 1950s. The large supply caused the market prices of gas to decline relative to the FPC's price ceilings. Prices started to increase in the late 1960s when producers no longer had a large inventory of undeveloped fields with which to respond to rising demand. With prices bumping against ceilings which were below the expected cost of finding and developing new fields, the producers had little incentive to explore for new supplies. Costs had increased but ceilings were stationary or moving upward more slowly than costs. The FPC was paddling upstream with a small paddle when it tried to react to the gas shortage. Its policy changes were late and of a short-run nature. They did little to change producers' long-run expectation that they would not be allowed protection against rising production costs and inflation through higher field-market gas prices.

This study shows that producers can be expected to respond to higher prices in long-term contracts, just as they did in the unregulated field market of the years before 1960. The current increase in drilling activity is in response to the higher prices recently allowed by the FPC for interstate sales, the higher prices in the unregulated intrastate market, and the anticipation that long-term interstate prices will be even higher when the field market is deregulated. This increased exploration will result in more new gas supplies for the next few years. If the commission reestablishes firm price controls—albeit at a higher level than those of the past—new interstate commitments of gas can be expected to begin declining in the next few years just as they did in the past. There will be a continuous flow of new gas to the market to meet market demand only if producers are assured that they can earn a competitive return on their investment.

Suggestions for Reducing the Cost of Regulation in the Absence of Complete Deregulation

Several proposals before the Congress, including that of the Nixon administration,[7] would deregulate "new" gas to be committed under

---

[7] President's Energy Message to Congress, April 18, 1973, House Document No. 93-85. The President proposed "that the gas from new wells, gas newly dedicated to interstate markets, and the continuing production of natural gas from expired contracts should no longer be subject to price regulation at the wellhead."

future interstate contracts but not "old" gas already committed. The detrimental effects of this compromise approach on gas prices and supply have been discussed above. However, these detrimental effects could be reduced if the decontrol legislation explicitly stated that the cutoff date between old and new gas would not be changed at a later time. This would give producers some assurance that Congress would not subsequently extend price controls to whatever gas may have been committed to the interstate market in the interim. And it would help reduce producer uncertainty about future FPC policy.

In the absence of congressional decontrol, there are several steps the FPC could take to reduce the cost that field market regulation places upon society.[8] The most obvious one would be to set a new nationwide price-ceiling sharply above the current level. However, given its statutory responsibility to "protect consumers from higher prices," the commission would not be able to deregulate the market fully through this procedure. The new ceiling would have to be low enough to be binding on most producers in higher-cost areas and areas closer to retail markets, but high enough so as not to be binding on most producers in the major southwest producing areas (including the Gulf of Mexico). Given current prices for unregulated intrastate gas, it appears that the FPC's new nationwide rate of 42¢/Mcf (even with some fixed escalation and allowances included) will still be binding in most producer areas.

Higher nationwide ceilings, however, can never substitute for complete deregulation. A nationwide ceiling set above the market prices prevailing in most areas would duplicate the situation producers faced in the mid-1960s under area-rate controls. If market prices should again increase, as they did during the 1967-69 period, the nationwide price ceiling could again become binding in the major low-cost producing areas. In that event, the FPC could be expected to move slowly, just as it did in the past. Thus, in the absence of congressional decontrol, consumers might once more be faced with inadequate supplies of gas resulting from producer uncertainty about FPC policy.

Other measures are available to the FPC to help overcome the effects upon producers of anticipated inflation. First, the use of indefinite escalation clauses in natural gas contracts should be reinstituted. These clauses could allow price changes based on changes in the consumer or wholesale price index. Such clauses

---

[8] See the discussion in Chapter 2 on FPC action already taken.

were developed in the late 1940s and 1950s in response to the effects of inflation and state taxation but were made inoperative by the FPC in 1961 (see page 15). Now that the rate of inflation has increased, there is every reason to believe that anticipated inflation has a strong detrimental effect on producer decisions to make long-term commitments to the gas market.

Second, the certification of shorter-term contracts should be permitted. The commission was doing this to a limited extent by allowing pipelines to make "emergency" and limited-term purchases of gas at prices above established area rates. All other things being equal (including price), a producer should be more willing to commit a quantity of gas to the interstate market for a short period (say five years) than for a long period (the traditional twenty years). A short-term contract would reduce producer uncertainties about future prices, costs, and regulatory policy. Even with a binding ceiling rate, interstate pipelines would be able to purchase a larger quantity of gas for annual delivery with short-term contracts than with long-term contracts.

Concluding Comment

Using a model derived from the behavior of producers in an unregulated market, this study has shown the effects and consequences of this country's long-term effort to improve social welfare by regulating the field price of natural gas. Some consumers may have gained as a result of lower field prices, although they, too, will lose as distribution companies are forced to employ much higher cost LNG and SNG to replace dwindling reserves. Nevertheless, given the existence of the current natural gas shortage, FPC rationing, a reduced inventory of proven reserves, and large gains to regulated pipelines, the policy cannot be termed a success. It failed despite the good intentions of the congressmen who voted for the Natural Gas Act of 1938, of the Supreme Court justices who extended the regulation in 1954, and of the FPC commissioners and staff who have attempted to implement the regulation. Their error was not in being insincere about the well-being of consumers, but in failing to comprehend the implications of Adam Smith's famous statement:

> As every individual endeavours as much as he can both to employ his capital in the support of domestic industry, and so to direct that industry that its produce may be of the greatest value; every individual necessarily labours to render the annual revenue of the society as great as he can.

He generally neither intends to promote the public interest, nor knows how much he is promoting it. . . . he intends only his own gain, and he is in this led by an invisible hand to promote an end which was no part of his intention. . . . By pursuing his own interest he frequently promotes that of the society more effectually than when he really intends to promote it.[9]

Those who wanted to protect consumers through natural gas regulation may have had good intentions—but that is what the road to hell is paved with. The problem of monopoly exploitation of consumers never existed in the field market and was probably greatly exaggerated for the pipeline industry. Indeed, there is strong evidence that the monopoly and monopsony power of pipelines has been significantly increased by FPC regulation itself. Perhaps it is time to question not only the prescription of regulation, but the original diagnosis of monopoly power which brought it about. People who see ghosts in all dark places may be afraid of the dark. The cure may be not to create a bureaucratic monster to chase away the ghosts, but to shed more light on the dark places.

---

[9] Adam Smith, The Wealth of Nations (Modern Library edition), p. 423.

APPENDIX

Appendix A: The Testing Model and Its Results [1]

The basic testing procedure is to compare actual price and quantity data for the years after area-rate controls were begun with yearly predictions of price and quantity based on the performance of the industry before the change. The preregulation performance has been summarized by multiple regression estimates of a distributed-lag supply model.

Four different supply relationships are estimated—the first for the annual change in the total stock of reserves, the second for additions to reserves from exploration and development activity, the third for reserves added by exploration activity only, and the fourth for the amount of exploratory well drilling. This procedure reflects the current classification of published natural gas reserve data and a belief that some of the less refined measures of reserve additions contain large random components.

The four equations used to estimate the supply function before the initiation of regulation are

$$R_t = \pi_o + \pi_1 PG + \pi_2 PO + \pi_3 PL + \pi_4 R_{t-1} + u_{t1}, \tag{1}$$

$$NDXR_t = \lambda_o + \lambda_1 PG_t + \lambda_2 PO_t + \lambda_3 PL_t + \lambda_4 R_{t-1}$$
$$+ \lambda_5 (QF_t - S_t) + u_{t2}, \tag{2}$$

$$ND_t = \Phi_o + \Phi_1 PG_t + \Phi_2 PO_t + \Phi_3 PL_t + \Phi_4 R_{t-1}$$
$$+ \Phi_5 (QF_t - XR_t - S_t) + u_{t3}, \tag{3}$$

$$F_t = \Psi_0 + \Psi_1 PG_t + \Psi_2 PO_t + \Psi_3 PL_t + \Psi_4 F_{t-1} + u_{t4}, \tag{4}$$

---

[1] For a more detailed development of the model and a discussion of the data and results, see Helms, *The Effectiveness of FPC Regulation*, Chapter 4.

where

R_t = the *stock* of reserves in year t;

ND_t = new discoveries in year t;

XR_t = extensions plus revisions in year t;

$NDXR_t = ND_t + XR_t$;

F_t = the stock (that is, the sum of all past drilling of successful [dry holes are excluded] gas exploratory drilling as of year t);

PG_t = new contract price of natural gas in year t;

PO_t = the price of crude oil in year t;

PL_t = the price of natural gas liquids in year t;

QF_t = the quantity of gas produced (extracted) from reserves in year t;

S_t = the net change in storage in year t;

u_{ti} = disturbance terms;

π_i, λ_i, Φ_i and Ψ_i = regression coefficients estimated by ordinary least squares.[2]

By including the lagged values of reserves (R_{t-1}) or footage drilled (F_{t-1}), the distributed lag model attempts to estimate how producers responded by adjusting their actual level of reserves (or drilling footage) to the level they would have desired. It is a basic premise of the model that the adjustment process of actual to desired stock from one year to the next is not complete. This premise is realistic for the oil and gas producing industry since it usually takes from one to six years for the output of reserves to respond to economic stimuli. In this model the economic stimuli which influence producers' decisions about exploration and development drilling (and hence their idea of the "desired" stock of reserves) are taken to be the price of new gas (PG), the price of crude oil (PO), and the price of natural gas liquids (PL).

The estimation of equations (2) and (3) uses the available breakdown of natural gas data to concentrate more closely on producers' decisions with respect to exploration drilling (3) and exploration and development drilling (2). The procedure removes from the dependent variable some of the categories of natural gas data (QF, S, XR) which are thought to contain large random variations not directly controllable by producers. For example, equa-

---

[2] By American Gas Association (AGA) annual accounting procedure,
$$R_{t-1} + ND_t + XR_t - QF_t + S_t \equiv R_t.$$

tion (3) estimates how producers responded to changing prices in a free market by adjusting their exploratory drilling for new gas. The output of their exploratory drilling is deemed to be new discoveries.

After these four equations are estimated, the values of the coefficients (π), (λ), (Φ), and (Ψ) are used to make post-regulation estimates of $\hat{R}$, $\hat{NDXR}$, $\hat{ND}$, and $\hat{F}$ respectively. These estimates of producer response in the absence of regulation are made in the following way. The actual 1961-69 values of PO and PL are multiplied by their respective coefficients since it is assumed that FPC regulation did not affect these variables. But since FPC regulation took the form of a price freeze, a different procedure must be used to obtain estimates of unregulated natural gas prices. To obtain these estimates, a "reduced-form" model of the following type is estimated for the preregulation period:

$$PG_t = z_0 + z_1 RQD_t + z_2 PO_t + z_3 PL_t + v_t. \qquad (5)$$

The new variable, RQD_t, is the yearly quantity of gas reserves demanded in the field. It is a derived demand variable depending upon the rate of growth of gas markets.[3] Through the use of exogenous data for RQD_t, PO_t, and PL_t, a series of "unregulated" prices (PGFIT) are estimated for the post-regulation period. These are multiplied by the price coefficients from the various supply equations (1 through 4) to obtain the estimates of supply response under unregulated conditions.

The results of the model are as follows:[4] The 1945-60 estimation of the reduced-form model (5) is

$$LOG\ PG = \underset{(3.80)}{3.79} + \underset{(0.16)}{0.15}\ LOG\ RQD_t$$

$$+ \underset{(3.10)}{1.70}\ LOG\ PO - \underset{(-4.12)}{1.93}\ LOG\ PL_t.$$

$$R^2 = .8187;\ F\text{-test} = 18.04\ ***$$

The values for PGFIT for the years 1961-69 projected by these coefficients are presented in Table A-1 along with actual values for PG for comparison. These results also appear in Figure 2 in the text.

---

[3] $RQD_t = 14.5\ (QF_t - QF_{t-1}) + QF_t.$

[4] The numbers in parentheses are the student's t-statistic; the F-test refers to a test of the null-hypothesis that all coefficients are equal to zero. The levels of confidence of 90, 95, 97.5 and 99 percent are designated by (*), (**), (***), or (****) respectively.

Table A-1

ACTUAL AND PROJECTED NEW CONTRACT PRICES, SEVEN SOUTHWEST STATES, 1961-69

(cents/million cubic feet)

Year	Actual Prices PG	Projected Prices PGFIT	Differences
1961	17.85	18.49	0.6
1962	17.40	18.97	1.6
1963	16.95	22.68	5.7
1964	16.12	22.36	6.2
1965	16.98	20.30	3.3
1966	16.43	18.74	2.3
1967	17.53	17.70	0.2
1968	17.48	22.91	5.4
1969	17.43	30.20	12.8

Note: Prices are deflated by the wholesale price index, 1957-59 = 100.
Source: Actual prices from Foster Associates, Inc.

The regression results obtained from estimating the supply equations (1), (2), (3), and (4) for the preregulation period are presented in Table A-2. The postregulation projections, which are the basis for Figures 3 through 6 in the text, appear in Tables A-3 and A-4.

Table A-2

DISTRIBUTED LAG REGRESSION RESULTS

(t-statistics in parentheses)

Equation	Years	Dependent Variable [Mean]	Constant	PG	PO	PL	Lagged Stock [c]	Y [d]	R²	F-test
(1)	1945-60	R [206.33] [a]	34.92 (3.07)	2.03 (3.07)	-1.21 (-0.27)	0.28 (0.17)	0.75 (8.92)		.9947	516****
(2)	1947-60	NDXR [16.39] [a]	42.82 (2.35)	2.14 (2.53)	-2.74 (-0.48)	2.72 (1.49)	-0.55 (-3.27)	5.67 (2.12)	.7779	5.60***
(3)	1947-60	ND [5.25] [a]	3.24 (0.36)	0.78 (1.80)	0.37 (0.15)	0.61 (0.77)	-0.06 (-1.19)	0.14 (1.18)	.6698	3.24*
(4)	1946-60	F [89.76] [b]	-0.05 (-0.09)	0.57 (1.25)	2.18 (0.70)	-0.38 (-0.35)	1.04 (37.91)		.9995	4998****

[a] In equation (1), (2), and (3), mean is in trillions of cubic feet.
[b] In equation (4), mean is in millions of feet drilled.
[c] Lagged stock is R_{t-1} in (1), (2), and (3), F_{t-1} in (4).
[d] In (2), $Y = QF - S$; in (3) $Y = QF - XR - S$.

Table A-3

ACTUAL AND PROJECTED RESERVES, 1961-69

(trillions of cubic feet)

Year	Actual Reserves R	Projected Reserves $\hat{R}$	Shortage [a]	Actual $ND+XR$	Projected $ND\hat{X}R$	Shortage	Actual ND	Projected $\hat{ND}$	Shortage
1961	266.3	266.7	.40	17.17	17.96	.79	6.908	6.242	−0.666
1962	272.3	270.9	−1.39	19.48	17.79	−1.69	6.299	6.027	−0.272
1963	276.1	281.5	5.32	18.16	26.90	8.74	5.578	8.536	2.958
1964	281.3	288.8	7.50	20.25	24.12	3.87	6.909	7.871	0.962
1965	286.5	290.1	3.68	21.32	20.64	−.68	6.544	5.865	−0.679
1966	289.3	288.2	−1.17	20.22	22.71	2.49	6.058	4.746	−1.312
1967	292.9	284.6	−8.31	21.80	22.88	1.08	5.695	3.812	−1.883
1968	287.3	292.4	5.00	13.70	35.53	21.83	2.922	8.240	5.318
1969	275.1	312.8	37.70	8.38	48.32	39.94	3.813	14.712	10.899

[a] Discrepancies due to rounding of R and $\hat{R}$.

Source: Actual data from AGA, *Monthly*, vol. 52, no. 5 (May 1970), p. 7.

Table A-4

ACTUAL AND PROJECTED CUMULATED EXPLORATORY WELL FOOTAGE, 1961-69
(millions of feet)

Year	Actual Footage F	Projected Footage $\hat{F}$	Shortage $\hat{F} - F$
1961	226.9	226.8	−0.1
1962	247.6	250.1	2.5
1963	265.5	276.6	11.1
1964	283.9	303.8	19.9
1965	303.1	330.7	27.6
1966	324.4	357.6	33.2
1967	340.8	384.9	44.1
1968	360.8	416.3	55.5
1969	381.8	453.4	71.6

Source: Actual data from *AAPG Bulletin,* June issues, 1962-70.

Appendix B: Computation of the Cost of Domestic versus Imported Gas Supplies

The procedure for estimating unregulated new contract prices is to solve equation (1) for PG^* (an equilibrium price of gas) in the following manner:

$$PG^* = \frac{R_t}{2.03} - 17.20 + 0.60\,PO_t - 0.14\,PL_t - 0.37\,R_{t-1}.$$

By assuming a level of reserves desired at the end of each year (R_t), the model generates a vector of "equilibrium" new contract prices which can be used to compute the cost of new gas each year.[1] Each year's new contract price (PG^*) is averaged with new contract prices for the preceding ten years to obtain (P_{1t}), the average cost of consumption in year t. The desired level of reserves (R_t) is assumed to be ten times annual production $(R/Q = 10)$.[2] Annual production (consumption) in the initial year (1972) is assumed to be 26.113 Tcf as estimated by the Future Requirements Committee (FRC) and adjusted by the FPC.[3]

To incorporate a demand elasticity estimate in the computations, it is assumed that the FRC projections represent a pure income effect given current prices. By combining the FRC's annual percentage growth with the annual percentage change in price multiplied by an elasticity of demand estimate,[4] the net percentage change in annual consumption can be computed.[5] From this can be computed a new estimate of annual consumption $(Q_{1,t+1})$, a new target

---

[1] PO_t is assumed to remain at \$10 per barrel from 1974 through 1980. PL_t is assumed to increase at an annual rate of 3 percent.

[2] For the contiguous United States, the R/Q ratio for 1972 was 10.5 (AGA, *Reserves*, 1972, Table I).

[3] FPC, *Supplies of Natural Gas Pipeline Companies*, Table 15, p. 118.

[4] MacAvoy's demand elasticity estimate of -2.2 is taken as the long-run demand elasticity. Paul W. MacAvoy, "The Effectiveness of the Federal Power Commission," *The Bell Journal of Economics and Management Science*, vol. 1, no. 2 (Autumn 1970), p. 295. In order to account for consumers' gradual adjustment to higher prices, it is assumed that the elasticity of demand increases from a relatively inelastic -0.5 in 1972 to the long-run elasticity of -2.2 by 1980.

[5] Where Q is actual consumption, N the net change in consumption, Q' the quantities predicted by the FRC, and η the elasticity of demand

$$N = \frac{Q'_{t+1} - Q'_t}{Q'_t} + \eta \left(\frac{P_t - P_{t-1}}{P_{t-1}} \right)$$
$$(N + 1)Q_t = Q_{t+1}.$$

This procedure assumes there is a one-year lag in consumers' response to a price change.

level of reserves ($R_{t+1} = 10\ Q_{1,t+1}$), a new equilibrium price (PG^*_{t+1}) from the equation above, and a new average price ($P_{1,t+1}$), and so on.

The procedure for obtaining P_2 and Q_2 is similar, except that in this case it is assumed that the FPC maintains a ceiling price for new gas of 26¢ throughout the period.[6] With a given new contract price, the level of reserves is obtained directly from equation (13). Imports are assumed to be whatever amount of gas is required to keep domestic reserves equal to ten times annual consumption.

---

[6] For consistency with the estimation coefficients, all computations were carried out using constant 1957-59 dollars. However, the results are presented in 1973 constant dollars using the 1973 WPI of 154.16 (1957-59 = 100).

Cover and book design: Pat Taylor